WHISTLEBLOWING
AT WORK

CRIME AND SOCIETY

Series Editor
John Hagan, *University of Toronto*

Whistleblowing at Work: Tough Choices in
Exposing Fraud, Waste, and Abuse on the Job,
Terance D. Miethe

Losing Legitimacy: Street Crime and the Decline
of Social Institutions in America, Gary LaFree

Casualties of Community Disorder: Women's Careers
in Violent Crime, Deborah R. Baskin and Ira B. Sommers

Public Opinion, Crime, and Criminal Justice,
Julian V. Roberts and Loretta Stalans

Poverty, Ethnicity, and Violent Crime,
James F. Short

Great Pretenders: Pursuits and Careers of
Persistent Thieves, Neal Shover

Crime and Public Policy: Putting Theory to Work,
edited by Hugh D. Barlow

Control Balance: Toward a General Theory of Deviance,
Charles R. Tittle

Rape and Society: Readings on the Problems of Sexual Assault,
edited by Patricia Searles and Ronald J. Berger

WHISTLEBLOWING

AT WORK

*Tough Choices in Exposing Fraud,
Waste, and Abuse on the Job*

TERANCE D. MIETHE

WESTVIEW PRESS
A Member of the Perseus Books Group

Crime and Society

Copyright © 1999 by Westview Press, A Member of the Perseus Books Group

Published in 1999 in the United States of America by Westview Press, 5500 Central Avenue, Boulder, Colorado 80301-2877, and in the United Kingdom by Westview Press, 12 Hid's Copse Road, Cumnor Hill, Oxford OX2 9JJ

Library of Congress Cataloging-in-Publication Data
Miethe, Terance D.
    Whistleblowing at work : tough choices in exposing fraud, waste, and abuse on the job / by Terance D. Miethe.
        p.   cm. — (Crime and society)
    Includes bibliographical references and index.
    ISBN 0-8133-3549-3 (hc.)
    1. Whistleblowing.   2. Whistleblowing—United States—Case studies.   3. Administrative agencies—Corrupt practices—United States—Case studies.   4. Corporations—Corrupt practices—United States—Case studies.   I. Title.   II. Series: Crime & society (Boulder, Colo.)
HD60.5.U5M54   1999
331.2—dc21   98-43034
                                                                                       CIP

The paper used in this publication meets the requirements of the American National Standard for Permanence of Paper for Printed Library Materials Z39.48-1984.

10   9   8   7   6   5   4   3   2

Contents

Tables and Figures

Acronyms

B & W	Brown and Williamson Tobacco Company
CCSD	Clark County Public School District
CEO	chief executive officer
CHAMPUS	Civilian Health and Medical Program of the Uniform Services
CSRA	Civil Service Reform Act
DBE	Disadvantaged Business Enterprise
DFR	Duty of Fair Representation
DOD	Department of Defense
EEOC	Equal Employment Opportunity Commission
EPA	Environmental Protection Agency
ERISA	Employee Retirement Income Security Act
FBI	Federal Bureau of Investigation
FDA	Food and Drug Administration
FLSA	Fair Labor Standards Act
FMHSA	Federal Mine Health and Safety Act
GAO	General Accounting Office
GAP	Government Accountability Project
GATE	Gifted and Talented Education
HDPE	high density polyethylene
JTPA	Job Training and Partnership Act
LHWCA	Longshoreman's and Harbor Worker's Compensation Act
MTA	Metropolitan Transportation Authority
NLRA	National Labor Relations Act
NLRB	National Labor Relations Board
OSC	Office of Special Counsel

OSHA	Occupational Safety and Health Act
PETA	People for the Ethical Treatment of Animals
POGO	Project on Government Oversight
PSNS	Puget Sound Naval Shipyard
R&D	research and development
RA2	Restricted Area 2
RICO	Racketeering Influenced and Corrupt Organization Act
SOAR	Student Options for Academic Realization
STAA	Surface Transportation Assistance Act
STAND	Safe Texans Against Nuclear Disposal
TAF	Taxpayers Against Fraud
UFO	unidentified flying object
UTC	United Technologies Corporation
WBE	Women Business Enterprise
WPA	Whistleblower Protection Act

Preface and Acknowledgments

By all indications, the topic of whistleblowing has received growing attention in contemporary U.S. society. Across a variety of work settings, many employees observe misconduct at work and must face the difficult choice of either reporting it or remaining silent. Their act of whistleblowing is often associated with retaliation from both co-workers and management. Both federal and state laws have been enacted in the past two decades to provide some legal protection for whistleblowers in government, business, and industry.

Although whistleblowing has received wide attention in the mass media and public policy, little systematic research has been conducted on the extent of observing and reporting organizational misconduct, the social profile of whistleblowers, and the consequences of whistleblowing for the individual whistleblower, the work organization in which it occurs, and the wider society. The purpose of this book is to utilize the collection and analysis of various types of data to explore these fundamental questions about whistleblowing and summarize what we know about the experiences of whistleblowers. For employees contemplating the exposure of fraud, waste, or abuses in their workplace, this book provides a detailed summary of the current legal protection for whistleblowers against organizational reprisals and some general guidelines for reporting misconduct. By highlighting the typical patterns for whistleblowers, the material presented here may provide readers with the knowledge to make more informed judgments about whether or not to report organizational misconduct.

Several people have played a major role in the development of my research interest in whistleblowing and the completion of this book. Joyce Rothschild at the Virginia Polytechnic Institute and State University has been a collaborator on several research papers on whistleblowing. Wayne Label at the University of Nevada–Las Vegas sparked my interest in the role of whistleblowing among auditors and was instrumental in providing the resources to conduct our national survey of auditors. Richard McCorkle has been an especially important colleague as a sounding board for my ideas about whistleblowing. Robert Meier has been a major force in the development of my understanding of organizational and occupational crime. Finally, I would like to thank Adina Popescu at Westview Press for her support and encouragement.

Terance D. Miethe

1

Introduction

U.S. workers observe fraud, waste, and abuse at work on a daily basis. Sexual harassment, employee theft, breaches of confidentiality, discriminatory employment practices, safety and health violations, consumer rip-offs, and financial frauds are both endemic to our society and a growing national epidemic. Consider what some ordinary citizens have seen at their workplaces in the past few years:

- Students in a "gifted" program receive personal computers and other high-tech equipment, but a teacher at the same public school can't get such basic educational equipment as dictionaries and pencils for her students because the district has no money. Many parents of the "gifted" children are high-level administrators or staff in the school district.
- A field engineer observes that the construction company he is working for failed to properly install a gas-proof membrane and uses insufficient amounts of reinforcement materials in the construction of a multi-billion-dollar subway tunnel.

- A television station employee is sexually harassed by her production manager and is discriminated against in a promotion decision.
- A nurse at a county hospital notices that her immediate supervisor is not following proper procedures for collecting and testing blood donations, risking the health of both patients and donors through the transmission of hepatitis and the AIDS virus.
- An administrative assistant, reviewing her financial records, discovers that county commissioners are using public funds to pay for their private automobiles and family vacations.
- Contrary to industry standards regarding the humane treatment of animals, a worker sees animals routinely skinned alive at a meat-processing plant.
- An air-cargo pilot notices that ground workers are not properly deicing airplanes before they depart in bad weather.
- An accountant discovers that the company manager is selling its product at below market value. The manager is receiving kickbacks in exchange for selling the product at the lower price.
- A maintenance worker at a company that produces highly explosive materials sees a co-worker smoking cigarettes in a restricted area.
- A clerical worker in a nonprofit organization observes another employee steal a computer from the office.

What would you do if you saw these activities? There are several options. You could do nothing, convincing yourself that it's none of your business, no harm is being done, or it's someone else's problem. Another option is to report it directly to your immediate supervisor or to someone else within the company. How about going outside the company and reporting it to the police, district attorney, attorney general, or another governmental agency?

Unfortunately, before you choose a course of action, think about this: There are some clear advantages and numerous, often unexpected, disadvantages for each option. Whatever you do, it's a no-win situation.

Take "doing nothing" or what academics call being a "silent observer." Often considered the safest option, inaction is impossible for many workers because they are under a higher moral or legal obligation to report fraud, waste, and abuse. The failure to act is insubordination in the military and in other settings may result in civil or criminal charges for aiding and abetting, collusion, or conspiracy. When inaction results in serious injury or death to other people (as happened in the example of improper blood testing), you may suffer lifelong guilt and psychological distress. Even when the consequences to others are less severe, silent observers often report deep regret and remorse for not speaking out.

Reporting misconduct to an official within the company is an equally unattractive option. Some employers may offer small perks (like a pat on the back or a small bonus) for helping the company identify "bad apples" or avoid negative publicity. However, at the same time that praise is given for your efforts, management will often chastise you privately for being a "squealer" and define you as an untrustworthy and dangerous employee. The reasoning behind their negative evaluations is simple: Persons willing to snitch on friends and co-workers will probably do the same upon discovery of more severe and systemic misconduct by the corporation itself. If you are considered the company spy or snitch, your relationship with fellow workers will also deteriorate as a result of speaking out.

Finally, you could go totally outside the company and report the misconduct to an external agent—police, attorney, news reporter, regulatory agent, government official. Here, the outcome and consequences are also unattractive. Unless you are totally indispensable to the organization (for instance, married to the chief executive officer or possessing skills that can't be replaced), your act of defiance of company norms by "airing dirty laundry" is often professional suicide and usually results in swift, certain, and severe forms of organizational retaliation. You could lose your job (or be forced to resign because the company has made your life totally miserable), co-workers may shun and avoid you, other employers may blacklist you from receiving similar jobs, and severe economic and psychological harm may haunt you for the rest of your life. Of course, you may be entitled to financial compensation for being illegally fired or demoted, but taking legal action to be reinstated is expensive and time consuming, and legal judgments typically favor the company rather than the employee.

So, what did these ordinary people do and what happened to them? Here's a summary:

- The *teacher* wrote a letter to state legislators about running a private school within a public institution. When it became known that she had "gone public," she was dismissed in the middle of the semester. She subsequently filed a lawsuit against the school district for denying her First Amendment rights to "free speech," was awarded more than $100,000 in the lawsuit, and was ultimately reinstated to her teaching position. However, she now suffers from stress-related medical problems and has totally lost faith in other people and social institutions.

- The *construction engineer* reported the shoddy construction practices to numerous local, state, and federal agencies. He was fired from his job (presumably because of a reduction-in-force necessity) but has continued the fight for the last eight years to expose the deficiencies and force the company to take major corrective action. He has recently filed a state lawsuit, seeking monetary compensation for exposing this major problem. Although the experience has left deep financial and psychological scars, he has received some vindication from the growing public recognition of the construction flaws and the major health hazards posed by this public works disaster.

- After filing a complaint against the manager for sexual harassment, the *television employee* was denied the opportunity to apply for an advanced position within the station. Management claimed that she was a troublemaker and an incompetent worker (contrary to her written performance evaluations). She feels totally victimized by the experience and has now filed a lawsuit against the station for sex discrimination.

- The *nurse* questioned her supervisor on the inappropriate blood-testing procedures but nothing was changed for several weeks. As a consequence, at least three patients contracted the AIDS virus, and two of them have died from AIDS-related complications. Feeling personally responsible for not being more assertive with the incompetent supervisor, the nurse quit her job and now works at a hospice for terminally ill people. Lawsuits have been filed against the small county hospital where the tainted blood donations were collected. Fearful of physical threats made by local residents and co-workers, who will lose their jobs if her lawsuit is successful, the nurse was forced to leave town.

- Concerned about being falsely implicated with the county commissioners for misappropriation of public funds, the *administrative assistant* contacted an attorney and was advised to involve federal law enforcement officials. She wore a "wire" to get the commissioners' admission of wrongdoing and taped the offer of a $10,000 bribe for her silence by one of the commissioners. After four officials were indicted and pleaded guilty, the administrative assistant took another job and moved out of town. She feels good about what she did, but she was very concerned about retaliation while still living in the small town.

- The *meat-packing worker* reported the animal abuse on several occasions to his manager, but nothing was done. His superior said something like "Hey, they are only dumb animals—no big deal!" The worker was a college student, trying to make a few extra bucks on a part-time basis. He thought about reporting the abuse to PETA (People for the Ethical Treatment of Animals) or another animal-rights group, but he decided it wasn't worth it. Several weeks later, he went back to school.

- The *air-cargo pilot* was a new employee at the company when he observed the poor deicing efforts. He remained silent about the incident and other dubious practices because he didn't want to create any problems. He left the company for another job shortly after the episode. In retrospect, the pilot feels some guilt for not reporting the safety violations to aviation authorities.
- The *accountant* confronted the company manager about the price kickbacks and then reported the practice to the company stockholders. Lacking direct evidence of the manager's fraud (such as canceled checks), only about half of the stockholders believed the accusations. After continuing to work for several months in a now hostile and high-stress work environment, the accountant received a medical disability, retired, and left town. The accountant says that he doesn't talk about the incident, but it is clear that this experience dramatically altered his life.
- The *maintenance worker* reported the smoking incident to his supervisor. Because unauthorized smoking had previously caused a major explosion that killed two employees at the same plant, the offending employee was fired, and the maintenance worker was praised by management for his action.
- After the *clerical worker* reported the computer theft to her boss, the employee was asked to return the equipment and was subsequently fired. Formal crim-

inal charges, however, were not filed against the thief, possibly to minimize any negative publicity about misconduct within the nonprofit organization. The clerical worker was neither praised nor criticized by management for her actions. A replacement was hired after the incident, and things quickly returned to normal.

As illustrated by these examples, reactions to misconduct are wide and varied. Some people feel no major compulsion to speak out, and their organizations seem content with this inaction. Other employees become strongly committed to disclosing the abuse to authorities outside the organization and take whatever steps are necessary even in the face of severe and swift organizational retaliation. What individual, organizational, and situational factors account for these differences? And how can employees in a variety of work settings best respond to organizational misconduct without getting burned?

If your experiences are like those of other employees, the decision to "blow the whistle" will have lasting consequences. In fact, whistleblowing—the reporting by employees and former employees of illegal, unethical, and otherwise inappropriate conduct to someone who has the power to take corrective action—is often associated with marital conflict and family disruption, declines in psychological well-being, alienation from co-workers, short- and long-term financial distress, and a diminished faith and trust in other people and major social institutions.

Using data from personal interviews and surveys of employees in various work settings, this book examines whistleblowing and its individual and organizational consequences. Chapter 2 begins with a definition of whistleblowing, identifying its major forms, and describes the problems with studying whistleblowers. Special attention is given to isolating the key aspects and unique features of whistleblowing as a form of snitching. Chapter 3 describes the emergence of whistleblowing as a primary method for the detection and control of organizational misconduct. Available data on the prevalence of illegal activity at work, and alternative methods for controlling it, are also reviewed.

The extent of whistleblowing and its correlates—that is, the social and psychological attributes of whistleblowers, the situational factors, and the organizational characteristics that increase or decrease the likelihood of its occurrence—are covered in Chapter 4. Subsequent chapters examine the individual and organizational consequences of whistleblowing (Chapter 5), the legal rights and safeguards for whistleblowers (Chapter 6), and case histories of particular whistleblowers (Chapter 7). The concluding chapter provides a summary of strategic choices and practical advice for persons who are considering whether and how to report organization misconduct. The appendix provides a listing of support services for whistleblowers.

2

What Is Whistleblowing and How Do We Study It?

Most of the people described in the Introduction are whistleblowers. Except for the airline pilot who remained silent, the others are designated as "whistleblowers" because they are *employees or former employees who report misconduct to persons who have the power to take action* (see Miethe and Rothschild 1994; Miceli and Near 1992). Although this definition is fairly general, it is important to recognize that whistleblowing has come to mean so many different things to different people that it defies an unambiguous description. Widely used synonyms such as "snitches," "squealers," "rats," "moles," "finks," "stools," "blabbermouths," "tattletales," "ethical resisters," and "people of conscience" clearly illustrate our diverse perceptions of whistleblowers in U.S. society.

Definitional Issues

The general definition of whistleblowing used here includes basic elements and implies several other factors that distinguish it from other forms of snitching. The basic elements of whistleblowing and its unique aspects are described below.

The Office Snitch

A starting point for defining whistleblowers is to consider them the "office snitch." This short phrase, although highly pejorative, nonetheless captures two crucial aspects of whistleblowing: (1) its social acceptability and (2) where it occurs.

Let's first examine the social acceptance of whistleblowing. The two extreme positions are represented by the "snitch" and the "savior." As a snitch, the whistleblower is considered a lowlife who betrays a sacred trust largely for personal gain. When the betrayal occurs among children, the snitch is the tattletale or fink. The snitch who divulges intimate secrets about friends is called the "gossip," whereas the snitch who receives financial payment or other direct benefits from exposing "dirt" is the informant. The prison snitch is the "rat," and the "mole" is the company snitch who is planted by the organization itself. Whistleblowers are unique snitches in that their disclosures involve organizational misconduct, occur within the work setting, and are not necessarily supported by the organization (as is true of moles). From this perspective, the whistleblower is the office snitch.

Although often overlooked and minimized, a positive side exists for each type of snitching. In other words, the snitch can also be a "savior." By telling a parent that the neighbor's kid is lighting firecrackers without adult supervision, for example, the tattletale averts a serious injury.

The gossip who tells of another's amorous interests or abusive history may help a friend make the right decision. The rat helps prison officials maintain order within their institutions. Paid informants may help apprehend and convict serious and dangerous offenders. Similarly, the actions of nationally renowned whistleblowers such as Frank Serpico, Karen Silkwood, and "Deep Throat" ultimately lead to major changes in formal organizations, industry, and politics.

Whether whistleblowers are viewed as snitches or saviors depends, of course, on one's perspective. Richard Nixon, for example, probably didn't consider the anonymous "Deep Throat" a public savior. Nor did the officers exposed by the charges of mass corruption made by Frank Serpico against the New York Police Department or tobacco industry officials upon the disclosures by Dr. Jeffrey Wigand of the manipulation of nicotine levels in cigarettes. As discussed in detail later, the public image of whistleblowers as snitches or saviors and the social acceptability of this practice depends on how it is done and a variety of other factors. Nonetheless, whistleblowers are more typically viewed as snitches than public saviors even when their actions contribute to the greater good of a society.

The second important aspect of the label "office snitch" is that it implies that whistleblowing occurs in the context of work. What this means is that whistleblowers can only be employees or former employees of the organization where the misconduct takes place. Almost anyone can be a tattletale, gossip, mole, rat, or paid informant, but whistleblowers are unique because they face both public criticism for snitching and often strong pressure from their company to remain quiet. People may lose friends for being a tattletale or gossip. However, whistleblowers—along with the mole and rat—run the added risk of losing their livelihoods and lives. The whistleblower's commitment to an organization and its co-workers places additional constraints on him or her. Other types of informants generally experience less severe consequences for their disclosures.

The Motivation for Whistleblowing

Much has been written about the motivations for whistleblowing (see Glazer and Glazer 1989; Jos, Tompkins, and Hays 1989; Miceli and Near 1992; Miethe and Rothschild 1994). Is whistleblowing a selfish and spiteful act motivated by greed and personal interests, or is it a selfless, altruistic act that is undertaken only at extraordinary personal costs? In other words, does the self-serving office snitch or the self-sacrificing public savior best characterize the whistleblower?

Social scientists disagree on whether egoism or altruism is the ultimate motivation for whistleblowing and on whether the term *whistleblower* should be restricted to only altruistic acts (Glazer and Glazer 1989; Jos, Tompkins, and Hays 1989; Miceli and Near 1992). However, this debate is of limited practical value for a fundamental reason: Most whistleblowers themselves are unable to say whether their action is either personally or socially motivated. Their behavior is probably a little of both. When asked in interviews "What motivated or compelled you to report this act?" the respondent will usually say one thing ("It was the morally right thing to do") but later in the interview will invariably convey a different motivation ("The boss was a sniveling bastard so I nailed him!").

For purposes of exposing and controlling corruption at work, the motive for reporting is largely irrelevant as long as employees speak out. The importance of the stereotypical view of whistleblowers as self-serving snitches, however, is that it may discourage other employees from reporting misconduct at work and subsequently restrict the potential societal benefits from whistleblowing.

The motivations for whistleblowing become especially important when examining our reactions to whistleblowers. Whistleblowers who engage in altruistic acts at greater personal costs are often considered cultural heroes, whereas those motivated by greed and revenge are typically viewed as dirty, rotten scoundrels.

Staying Inside or Going Outside the Company

Whistleblowers are often distinguished according to the nature of their disclosures. There are two general types. "Internal" whistleblowers report misconduct to another person within the company who can take corrective action. This contact person may be an immediate supervisor, ombudsman, union representative, or company executive. "External" whistleblowers, in contrast, expose fraud, waste, and abuse in organizations to outside agents. Common sources for external reporting are law enforcement officials, lawyers, news media, and an assortment of local, state, and federal agencies. Both internal and external whistleblowers must resort to their action because they lack the power themselves to directly change organizational practices. Although a boss can fire an employee who steals company funds, whistleblowers must rely upon others to take corrective measures.

Whether internal reporting of misconduct qualifies as whistleblowing has been subject to debate. Several authors follow popular conceptions of whistleblowing and restrict it to the external disclosure of misconduct (see Glazer and Glazer 1989; Petersen and Farrell 1986). Other authors adopt a more inclusive definition that incorporates both internal and external reporting (Jos, Tompkins, and Hays 1989; Miceli and Near 1992; Miethe and Rothschild 1994).

Both internal and external reporting are included here as whistleblowing for two reasons. First, internal whistleblowing is often regarded as a precursor to external whistleblowing. Second, it is widely assumed that internal reporting elicits fewer negative reactions from both the public and the organization. Under these conditions, the inclusion of both internal and external forms of whistleblowing enables researchers to better ascertain the causal importance of individual, situational, and organizational factors in explaining the likelihood of whistleblowing and its consequences to the individual and the organization.

The Precipitating Misconduct

A wide variety of misconduct may precipitate or trigger the act of whistleblowing. Relatively minor personnel disputes, petty rule violations by co-workers, and more severe and systemic forms of misconduct by the company itself may all provide the "spark" for whistleblowing. A common stereotype of whistleblowing is that it involves the external reporting of frequent and severe corporate corruption that results in enormous financial loss or public harm. Actually, any type of misconduct, no matter how trivial or severe, may initiate the process of whistleblowing.

Role-Prescribed Behavior

There is some debate about whether persons whose daily work involves the reporting of misconduct (such as quality control personnel, security officers, internal auditors) are whistleblowers. Typically, these employees are not considered whistleblowers because (1) their reporting is expected or mandated by their particular occupational role and (2) they do not experience the same antagonism and condemnation for reporting misconduct. Only when these employees report misconduct outside proper channels (for instance, "leaking" information to the press or external federal authorities) does their behavior constitute whistleblowing. There may be some professional or ethical rules of conduct for reporting misconduct in various occupations, but whistleblowing is not part of one's everyday work role. In fact, whistleblowers are often novice snitches whose inexperience may contribute to their inability to change organizational practices or to handle subsequent retaliatory attacks by the organization.

How to Identify and Study Whistleblowers

Given the definition of whistleblowers as "employees or former employees who report organizational misconduct to persons who have the power to take action," how do we go about identifying and studying them? Because there is no readily available list of whistleblowers, researchers have resorted to several other strategies for identifying them.

One common approach involves the search of newspaper and magazine articles to select whistleblowers who have received media attention. The problem with this approach is that it focuses exclusively on high-profile cases of external whistleblowing (for instance, the faulty O-rings for the *Challenger* space shuttle, the Tail-Hook military scandal, or Anita Hill's accusations against judge Clarence Thomas). Whistleblowing accounts that receive media coverage, by definition, are considered "newsworthy" and thus are unlikely to represent the more typical and less sensational whistleblowing situation.

Other researchers select whistleblowers from lists of persons who contact a particular support agency such as The Government Accountability Project (Glazer and Glazer 1989; Jos, Tompkins, and Hays 1989). Unfortunately, these studies are also limited because they do not allow direct comparisons between different types of whistleblowers (internal versus external reporters) and other types of employees within the same organization (such as persons who are "silent observers" or nonobservers of misconduct). By including both whistleblowers and nonwhistleblowers, general surveys of particular types of employees (such as nurses, federal workers, or auditors) are better designed to make substantive inferences about the factors that distinguish whistleblowers from other employees.

Data Sources for the Current Research

Over the last decade, I have worked with several colleagues on projects designed to study whistleblowing in a variety of work environments. The following data sources are used and analyzed in this book to arrive at substantive conclusions about whistleblowing and its consequences.

First, we completed more than two hundred telephone interviews (averaging ninety minutes each) and a comparable detailed, anonymous mail survey on a national sample of whistleblowers. The respondents were individuals who asked for additional information about Integrity International, a support group for whistleblowers developed by Donald Soeken that was profiled in a feature article in *Parade Magazine* in August 1991. Through the cooperation of Dr. Soeken, Dr. Joyce Rothschild and I were able to receive a list of potential whistleblowers and successfully interviewed and surveyed 216 of these people.

Second, personal interviews, telephone interviews, and anonymous surveys were completed with an additional eighty-three whistleblowers across the country. These persons contacted us directly after becoming aware of our research through public radio, newspaper articles, or public presentations about whistleblowing.

Third, questions about observing misconduct and whistleblowing were included in two other projects: (1) a national telephone survey of 634 employees (see Miethe and Rothschild 1993) and (2) a statewide telephone survey of 326 workers in Virginia (Bayer, Strickland, and Miethe 1992). Although whistleblowing was not the primary topic of interest in these studies, questions about observing and reporting organizational misconduct were included in them to provide general population estimates of the rate of whistleblowing among U.S. employees.

Fourth, I have analyzed data on the whistleblowing attitudes and experiences of more than thirteen thousand federal employees who were surveyed in 1992. The survey was sponsored by the U.S. Merit System Protection Board (see MSPB 1993). Analysis of these data provides information about the social profile of federal whistleblowers and the level and type of organizational retaliation for reporting fraud, waste, and abuse.

Fifth, a short mail survey was distributed to employees in various work settings. These respondents include 148 workers in a high-security manufacturing firm, 66 employees at a large petrochemical plant, 18 university staff who work in an administrative unit, 27 workers in a large bookstore, 147 registered nurses in the state of Nevada, 353 external auditors across the country, and 130 employees of nonprofit organizations. These industry-based surveys allow for direct comparisons across different types of employees to identify the individual, situational, and organizational characteristics that distinguish external whistleblowers from internal whistleblowers, silent observers, and nonobservers of misconduct.

Finally, I have reviewed previous research on whistleblowing to assess the consistency of conclusions across studies. A reference list of these past efforts is included in this book. When combined with the research findings of others, the data collected and analyzed here provide a strong basis for conclusions about whistleblowing and its consequences.

3

Snitching, Changing Work Organizations, and Whistleblowing

Whistleblowing is nothing new. Employees for centuries have observed and reported fraud, waste, and abuse in their workplace. However, our general attitudes toward whistleblowing and its importance in exposing misconduct have changed over time. In this chapter I examine these attitudes toward snitching and changes in work organizations that have increased the necessity of whistleblowing.

The Origins of Negative Attitudes Toward Snitching

Regardless of its particular form, snitching is widely condemned in U.S. society. Most Americans view "rats" and "moles" as lowlife in both the human and rodent worlds. What are the origins of these negative attitudes and has the social acceptance of snitching changed over time?

A primary source of the negative attitudes toward snitching is early childhood experiences. Children develop a negative view toward tattletales because they are often victim- ized by, and punished for, snitching. When children are "grounded" for conduct reported by a tattletale, they re- member it. They also remember that squealing is a way of losing friends. Gossip and other types of snitching are often viewed as betrayal and the violation of a sacred trust (Ak- erstrom 1991), further reinforcing their negative image. By telling their children to "mind their own business," parents also send the message that snitching is a devalued behav- ior. Given that early childhood socialization experiences in- fluence adult life, it isn't surprising that we carry a lot of negative baggage toward snitching that ultimately con- tributes to a general disapproval of whistleblowing. These negative images are maintained even though all of us have probably benefited at one time or another from snitching.

Another source of our views toward snitching is the mass media. Snitches are consistently viewed as sniveling lowlife in popular fiction, news reports, television, and film. The German spy placed in Stalag 18, the paid informants in television crime dramas like *NYPD Blue,* and the inmate "rat" in the Burt Reynolds movie *The Longest Yard* are all portrayed as distasteful subhumans. Coupled with our per- sonal experiences, these media images of snitches further promote a negative stereotype.

Among the different types of snitching, the public atti- tude toward whistleblowers is somewhat more positive. This is especially true of external whistleblowers who over- come major adversity to expose rampant organizational corruption that threatens public safety. However, negative attitudes toward whistleblowing may be quite similar to those held for other types of snitching because many people or their friends may have been victimized by the allegations of whistleblowers.

There is no definitive scientific data available that would allow us to determine whether the social acceptance and prevalence of whistleblowing and other types of snitching have changed over time. However, several observations and anecdotal accounts suggest that things have remained relatively stable over time. First, children today may call it different things ("narcing" or "ratting"), but they display the same general distaste for snitching as did their parents and grandparents. Second, special efforts and monetary incentives are still used to turn people into informants and whistleblowers, suggesting that normative proscriptions against snitching remain in contemporary society. Rather than report misconduct for its own intrinsic value, law enforcement officials must persuade confidential informants (through financial payment or immunity against prosecution) and other witnesses to speak out. If whistleblowing were more socially acceptable, financial and other incentives for disclosing misconduct, as well as hot lines and the passage of legislation to encourage whistleblowing, would be unnecessary. Third, the level of surveillance and monitoring has dramatically increased in contemporary society (Hodson and Sullivan 1995; Marx 1988), but this appears to have involved primarily electronic monitoring and other high-tech gadgets, rather than an increase in reporting by workers. Under these conditions, the prevalence and social acceptance of whistleblowing have changed little over the last several decades. Social norms toward meddling and "minding one's own business" are still firmly rooted in contemporary U.S. society.

What has changed over time, however, is society's need for whistleblowing. As described below, changes in work organizations and the nature of occupational and organizational misconduct have increased the importance of whistleblowing in the modern workplace.

Modern Work Organizations and the Need for Whistleblowers

The work world has gone through a major transformation in the last century. Workers in the late twentieth century produce more goods and a greater variety of goods than was ever before possible (Hodson and Sullivan 1995). Small, individually owned shops and trade stores have been replaced by large corporate entities with interlocking directorates and a massive hierarchical structure. Workers in the modern era rarely are involved in the total production process from the selecting of the raw materials to the finished product. Instead, modern work is piecemeal, fragmented, and specialized. The greater distancing of the worker from the final product, specialized tasks and areas of expertise, the invisible executive structure and absentee ownership in complex bureaucratic organizations, and the greater number of workers with direct involvement in the production process and service delivery have created a wider opportunity for illegal activity and more people to blame if something goes wrong.

The division of labor in modern industrial societies has resulted in the growth of specialized positions and greater vertical differentiation based on power. Workers whose tasks have now been finely subdivided in the modern workplace often experience diminished power because they have less control over the entire production or service activity (see Hodson and Sullivan 1995). This reduced power of workers to take their own corrective action may account for the greater reliance upon whistleblowing as a control measure in modern work organizations. In other words, if contemporary workers had greater control over the entire production and delivery process, there would be less need for whistleblowing.

Two examples are sufficient to illustrate these points about the changing workplace. Take, for instance, the food-processing industry and the health care delivery system. When I was in high school in the early 1970s, I worked as a butcher in a salmon-processing plant. There was only a two-person division of labor: the butcher and the "slimer"—the person who washed out the extra blood and slime missed by the butcher. By the early 1980s, this task became a three-person job, and now salmon butchering is automated in most plants, requiring about ten different specialized roles and functions on the assembly line. Under this production scheme (which is typical of nearly all food-processing industries), workers often take less pride in their finished product (because they are only partially re-sponsible for creating it), and there are greater risks of something going wrong in the process.

If you have had the misfortune of visiting a medical doc-tor in the last decade, you are no doubt acutely aware of the fragmented, specialized, and expertise-based health care delivery system in this country. The ratio of specialists to general practitioners has skyrocketed over the last three decades (*Statistical Abstracts of the United States* 1996). Now, the typical patient is referred to a nearly endless stream of specialists. In addition to impersonal treatment, increased costs, and a possible improvement in the overall quality of medical care, other consequences follow from this specialization in the medical profession. First, the opportunity for medical fraud and malpractice increases as more people become involved in the process of treatment. Second, medical abuses become more difficult to detect because knowledge of appropriate treatment is held by an increasingly small cadre of experts. Like the general problem with using company auditors and experts (rather than outside officials) to monitor organizational compliance to federal standards, the widespread use of only medical specialists to oversee the daily practices of other doctors is somewhat akin to having the fox guard the proverbial chicken coop.

Changes in the nature of modern work organizations are important because they reflect directly on the usefulness of whistleblowing as a mechanism of social control. Not only has knowledge become more specialized, but organizational practices are becoming increasingly private and distant from public scrutiny. In fact, often the only way to expose "office dirt" (such as fraud, waste, and abuse) in modern organizations is through disclosures by employees themselves. Without their willingness to become whistleblowers, we have limited means to either expose or control organizational misconduct (Miethe and Rothschild 1994).

Changes in Organizational and Occupational Deviance

Two general types of misconduct have plagued work organizations throughout history: organizational and occupational deviance. Organizational deviance (also called "corporate" crime) refers to criminal acts or violations of widely held moral and ethical standards that are committed to enhance the organization's position, power, and/or financial resources (see Coleman 1995; Friedrichs 1996). Bid-rigging and contract fraud, money laundering, illegal dumping of hazardous materials, price fixing, and cost-cutting activities that endanger the safety and health of workers are some examples of organizational deviance. In each case, particular individuals may benefit from the misconduct, but the behavior is supported by the organization and is functional for the continued operation of the company.

Occupational deviance, in contrast, involves criminal and unethical acts within a work setting that are motivated by individual needs and lack organizational support. Counterproductive work activities (such as substance abuse on the job, coming to work late or leaving early, taking unauthorized work breaks), prohibited personnel practices (such as discrimination and sexual harassment), financial frauds (such as embezzlement, overcharging for business expenses, falsifying time cards), and poor production or service activities (such as defrauding customers by low-quality service, abuse of clients) are examples of this type of misconduct. In contrast to organizational deviance (which is encouraged by company personnel), occupational deviance that results in only personal gains and harms corporate interests is not tolerated in most organizations (Mars 1982).

Although organizational and occupational deviance has occurred in companies throughout history, substantial changes in work organizations have altered the nature and detectability of both types of misconduct. Specifically, growing automation and technical expertise at work enhance criminal opportunities and provide a new modus operandi for crime. Employee theft and embezzlement, for example, now involve both somewhat crude liberations of company property (for instance, taking money from the till or clothes "off the rack") and more high-tech frauds (such as the use of dummy customer credit accounts). The dramatic rise in computer "hacking" from within and outside the company further illustrates the growing technical expertise of offenders (Miethe and Rothschild 1994).

The shift to more sophisticated and hard-to-detect crime is even more apparent for such organizational deviance as commercial fraud, price fixing, selling trade secrets, and the production of commodities that fail to meet specifications. Where complex accounting systems and regulatory guidelines are understood by only a few, there are numerous opportunities for unlawful and unethical behavior in modern work organizations (Miethe and Rothschild 1994). Other social forces, such as increased competition for scarce resources and the general weakening of corporate ethics in U.S. society, also provide a fertile climate for organizational abuse (Clinard 1983; Vaughan 1983). When individuals and corporations are sufficiently motivated to engage in workplace crime, the specialized and complex nature of much work activity provides some offenders with a near immunity against outside detection. Consider the difficulty in detecting the following organizational and occupational crimes:

- So-called data diddlers engage in computer-assisted embezzlement by manipulating to their advantage the information fed into computers. Funds intended for deposit in one account are credited to different accounts controlled by the criminals (Coleman 1994).
- "Collective embezzlement" is a scheme in which top managers siphon off company funds for their own personal use.
- Through secret files or "Trojan horses," computer programmers perform electronic transfers, erase personal debts, or discover confidential information without detection (Coleman 1994).
- Specific forms of medical fraud include "ping-ponging" (referring patients to several different practitioners when their symptoms do not warrant such referrals), "family ganging" (extending several unnecessary services to all members of a patient's family), "fee splitting" (sending patients to surgeons who will split the largest fee rather than to those who will do the best work), "steering" (directing patients to the clinic's pharmacies to fill unneeded prescriptions), and "upgrading" (billing for services more extensive than those actually performed) (Friedrichs 1996; Pontell, Jesilow, and Geis 1982).
- "Check-kiting" schemes are those in which financial institutions write checks for funds that have not yet been deposited and pocket the interest that is saved.

The brokerage house of E. F. Hutton pleaded guilty to using this scheme to get essentially interest-free loans by paying its bills with checks that were covered by other checks written on different banks, which were then covered by checks written on still other banks (Coleman 1994:89).

• "Stock parking" occurs when persons or corporations illegally conceal their ownership of stock in violation of securities law (Coleman 1994).

The Extent of Organizational and Occupational Deviance

Whistleblowing is essential for exposing misconduct in the modern workplace because organizational practices have become more complex, more specialized, and less publicly visible. But, how common is misconduct at work and how often is it observed by fellow employees?

It is difficult to gauge the true extent of organizational misconduct, but it is clearly a major problem in our society. Crude estimates of its prevalence and costs are simply staggering. Businesses are victimized by at least $5 billion per year from employee theft, and the public pays an additional 2 to 4 percent for retail merchandise to cover these losses (Coleman 1995; Friedrichs 1996). Thousands of Americans are killed each year by the manufacturing of unsafe products and the exposure of employees to illegal working conditions. The annual cost of antitrust violations such as illegal mergers, price fixing, and unfair cooperatives is more than $350 billion, the annual cost of tax fraud is nearly $300 billion, computer-related and high-tech crimes cost up to $200 billion, and the price tag for health-care fraud in Medicare and Medicaid is about $100 billion (Coleman 1995, 1994; Friedrichs 1996; Green 1990). When counterproductive work activities such as alcohol or drug use and skipping work are considered, national estimates of the prevalence of misconduct at work increase dramatically.

Although most organizational misconduct remains hidden and undetected, as does crime in general, survey results indicate that many Americans have directly observed a wide variety of abuses and inappropriate practices at work (see Table 3.1). In our national survey of 634 U.S. employees in 1993, over one-third of them had observed illegal or unethical practices at their company in the preceding two years. Nearly two-thirds of the sample of workers in business and industry in Virginia noted that they had observed some misconduct at work, ranging from health and safety violations (15 percent) to counterproductive work activities (55 percent). Almost half of the federal employees surveyed in 1981 said they observed illegal or wasteful activity in the last year, compared to only about one-in-five federal employees in 1992. Based on these estimates, it is clear that whistleblowing has enormous potential for exposing abuse and corruption in a variety of work settings.

Why Whistleblowing Is Needed to Control Organizational Misconduct

Social scientists have long debated the relative merits of various strategies for controlling occupational and organizational deviance (see Coleman 1995; Friedrichs 1996; Moore 1987). The conventional wisdom is that the white-

TABLE 3.1   Prevalence of Observing Misconduct Across
Different Studies

Study Description	% Observers[a]
National samples	
353 U.S. external auditors (Miethe and Label 1995)	56
634 U.S. employees (Miethe and Rothschild 1993)	37
8,592 federal workers (MSPB 1981)	45
4,897 federal workers (MSPB 1984)	25
13,309 federal workers (MSPB 1993)	17
State samples	
147 nurses in Nevada (Miethe 1994)	76
130 nonprofit employees in Nevada	
(Miethe and Rothschild 1995)	73
284 business/industry workers in Virginia	
(Rothschild and Miethe 1992)	65
1,212 nuclear industry workers in Tennessee	
(Blackburn 1988)	31
326 employees in Virginia	
(Bayer, Strickland, and Miethe 1992)	17
Averages across studies	44

[a] Numbers in this column represent the percentage of all workers
who observed different types of misconduct.

collar offender is guided by instrumental concerns such as
financial gain, has low commitment to crime as a lifestyle,
and weighs the relative costs and benefits when choosing
between criminal and conventional alternatives. Under
these conditions, people who commit acts for private gain
within organizations are commonly recognized as the most

deterrable types of offenders through the threat of swift, certain, and severe punishment. Because they have more to lose from a criminal conviction (their status, respectability, money, and comfortable life), corporate offenders, in particular, are assumed to be especially deterred by criminal sanctions (Miethe and Rothschild 1994). Both monetary fines and imprisonment are advocated for controlling occupational and organizational crime.

The major obstacle to deterring organizational misconduct, however, is the low probability of getting caught. In fact, offenders in work organizations maintain a near immunity against prosecution because of the low public visibility of much organizational crime, its technical complexity, and the strong pressures exerted on employees from both within and outside the organization to remain silent. Fellow employees, acting as whistleblowers, are uniquely situated to increase sharply the public visibility of organizational misconduct.

It may seem somewhat strange, but whistleblowing can reduce the likelihood of organizational misconduct even when it doesn't result in a criminal conviction or a civil finding of fault. In fact, for corporations that depend on the public's confidence and work hard at cultivating a clean image, the mere threat of public exposure from whistleblowers may be sufficient to curtail criminal activity. For example, look at how public donations for United Way plummeted when its former chief executive officer (CEO) was exposed for his extravagant air travel, exotic vacations, and hiring private limousine services on the company tab. The adverse publicity at United Way sent shock waves throughout nonprofit organizations across the country,

causing them to more closely monitor and curtail question-
able practices. In a world in which "image is everything,"
employees as potential whistleblowers have the inside
knowledge and subsequent power to increase accountability in many organizations.

Alternative Mechanisms for
Controlling Misconduct at Work

Occupational and organizational misconduct takes various
forms (some simple, some not), and these offenses vary
widely in their level of corporate support, the characteristics of the perpetrator(s), and the importance of the violation to the economic survival of the organization. Persons
who advocate whistleblowing and other strategies to control organizational misconduct must recognize this diver-
sity and develop options that are most effective under particular conditions. Two widely used alternatives to
whistleblowing are regulatory officials (such as inspectors
and auditors) and electronic surveillance.

External inspections and independent audits are mandated by law to monitor and regulate the operation of activities within many organizations and businesses. These
control activities vary in terms of their frequency (either
continuous or sporadic monitoring), scope, and the particular powers granted to the regulatory agents under administrative law. There is little doubt that inspections and external auditing have increased over the last several decades,
occurring at the same time that greater calls for accountability have been leveled at government, business, and industry. By regulating the type and nature of corporate ac-

tivities, inspections and audits have become an important fact of organizational life.

The effectiveness of these methods of social control, however, has been widely questioned on several grounds. For example, inspections and audits are often conducted on a sporadic or haphazard basis, allowing numerous opportunities for organizational noncompliance. In addition, the monitoring system may not be sufficiently fine-tuned to detect complex organizational misconduct, illegal transactions that may have been discovered by external auditors can be easily obscured by an alternative "paper trail," and many of these control activities take place well after the violation has occurred. These practices are further limited because regulators must rely upon the cooperation of the company, may identify more with company personnel with whom they work on a daily basis (rather than their own regulatory agency), and are fringe members who are often given a "sanitized" view of organizational practices.

Electronic surveillance by external agents and the use of paid informants are additional ways to detect and control organizational abuses. Spy kits are widely available for individual and corporate users to monitor various behaviors, ranging from cheating spouses to elaborate business transactions. Although both the technology for monitoring illegal transactions and the use of informants have dramatically increased over time (Marx 1988), these methods of controlling organizational behavior are also limited. In particular, they are restricted to the small number of organizations where agents have infiltrated or a magistrate has been convinced of "probable cause" before issuing a warrant for electronic surveillance and wiretapping. As fringe members of an organization, paid informants have less access to company records and private documents than persons who are more entrenched in the organizational hierarchy. These methods are also restricted to those organizations in which misconduct is already taking place, rather than being used to deter the onset of misconduct in the first place.

As a method for detecting and exposing misconduct in the workplace, whistleblowing has no rivals. Alternative methods are simply incapable of achieving the continuous monitoring and insights into organizational practices that are provided by employees themselves. In contrast to other methods of control, whistleblowers provide surveillance and monitoring in *all* organizations and are better situated in the organizational hierarchy to ask questions to build a solid case against offenders. Because it can be done immediately upon the detection of wrongdoing, whistleblowing may also be better able than other methods to stop organizational misconduct before it escalates. Although any comprehensive plan to detect and control organizational misconduct would include a variety of methods, the role of whistleblowing in this regard has only been recently recognized by academics, legislatures, and practitioners.

Summary

Changes in the structural features and production activities of modern work organizations and the growing sophistication of white-collar offenders have placed the burden of exposing illegal and unethical behavior squarely on the shoulders of whistleblowers. Electronic surveillance, external auditors, and paid informants are alternative methods of social control, but these approaches are simply unable to match up to the potential power of whistleblowers in exposing and controlling organizational practices. However, as described in later chapters, there are many personal, situational, organizational, and legal impediments to the disclosure of misconduct at work that may limit the likelihood and effectiveness of whistleblowing.

4

The Prevalence and the Profile of Whistleblowers

The previous chapter indicated that employees often observe misconduct at work. The questions addressed in this chapter are: (1) How often do employees report what they observe, and (2) what are the personal, situational, and organizational characteristics that influence the likelihood of being a whistleblower?

The Prevalence of Whistleblowing

Given strong societal norms about snitching, it is reasonable to expect that most people would remain quiet about organizational misconduct. The frequency of whistleblowing across different studies and different types of employees is summarized in Table 4.1. Rates of whistleblowing vary widely across these groups.

Almost two-thirds of the employees in our national survey who observed misconduct reported it. About one-half of the sample of all Virginia employees were whistleblowers compared to less than one-fourth of the workers in select businesses and industries in that state. Samples of spe-

TABLE 4.1   Rates of Whistleblowing and Types of Whistleblowers
Among Observers of Misconduct Across Different Studies

Study Description	% Whistleblowers[a]	% External Whistleblowers[b]
National samples		
892 directors of internal auditing (Near and Miceli 1988)	91	58
353 U.S. external auditors (Miethe and Label 1995)	87	25
634 U.S. employees (Miethe and Rothschild 1993)	62	16
13,309 federal workers (MSPB 1993)	51	32
4,897 federal workers (MSPB 1984)	31	na
8,592 federal workers (MSPB 1981)	30	14
State samples		
130 nonprofit employees in Nevada (Miethe and Rothschild 1995)	59	41
1,212 nuclear industry workers in Tennessee (Blackburn 1988)	58	na
147 nurses in Nevada (Miethe 1994)	52	15
326 employees in Virginia (Bayer, Strickland, and Miethe 1992)	48	25
284 business/industry workers in Virginia (Rothschild and Miethe 1992)	22	0
Averages across studies	54	24

[a] Numbers in this column represent the percentage of observers of misconduct who reported it.

[b] Numbers in this column represent the percentage of all whistleblowers who reported misconduct to external sources.

cific types of employees also yield wide estimates. Whistle-blowing was highest for directors of internal auditing (91 percent of observers of misconduct reported it), followed by external auditors (87 percent), workers in nonprofit organizations (59 percent), nuclear industry workers (58 percent), nurses (52 percent), and federal workers (ranging from 30 percent to 51 percent). The high whistleblowing rate among auditors is understandable given the behavior's status as largely role-prescribed behavior for these employees. The presence of codes of ethics that consider whistleblowing as behavior that promotes the greater good of society (often called "pro-social behavior") similarly helps explain the relatively high rates of whistleblowing among nonprofit employees and nurses. Across all studies combined, whistleblowing was the response for more than one-half of the observers of misconduct at work.

The majority of whistleblowers report misconduct only to family or close friends and persons within their organization. Most studies find that external reporting of misconduct to outside regulatory agencies, law enforcement personnel, or the mass media is done by less than one-fourth of all whistleblowers (see Table 4.1).

Although these data provide the best available estimates of the extent of whistleblowing, the derived estimates may be inflated for two reasons. First, employees are asked in most surveys only about their whistleblowing experience for the most serious misconduct they have observed. Because trivial violations of rules or laws are often given little attention, the emphasis on the most serious offense will overestimate the frequency of whistleblowing. Second, respondents to survey inquiries on the topic of whistleblowing are probably overrepresented by employees with more experience with organizational misconduct and/or stronger attitudes about reporting it. Even with the possible inflation, however, these studies clearly indicate that whistleblowing is a fact of modern organizational life and that external reporting of fraud, waste, and abuse is the major exception, rather than the rule, in most work settings.

The three national surveys of federal employees conducted by the U.S. Merit System Protection Board provide a rare opportunity to assess changes in observing misconduct and whistleblowing over time. Several patterns are revealed in these data (see Table 4.2). First, the proportion of federal workers who have observed misconduct at work has decreased dramatically, from nearly half in 1981 to less than one out of every five workers in 1992. Two plausible explanations for this decrease are that there is now less misconduct in federal work settings or that offenders have become more sophisticated and their misconduct is harder to detect by other workers. Second, the proportion of observers who are whistleblowers nearly doubled between 1981 and 1992, and rates of external whistleblowing more than doubled over that time period.

There are at least two possible explanations for the dramatic rise in external whistleblowing among federal workers over time. First, increases in external reporting may be a direct consequence of a growing frustration and disenchantment with internal remedies and reporting avenues. Second, federal workers' increased awareness of their legal rights as whistleblowers and enhanced financial incentives for reporting fraud against the government may also have increased rates of external whistleblowing. Information

TABLE 4.2   Trends in Observing and Reporting Misconduct
Among Federal Employees over Time

Characteristic by Year of Study	% of All Federal Workers
Observed misconduct at work?	
1981	45
1984	25
1993	17
Reported observed misconduct?	
1981	30
1984	31
1993	51
Whistleblowers who reported externally?	
1981	14
1993	32

Source: MSPB (1981, 1984, 1993)

about whistleblower protection, however, has not trickled down to most federal employees. In fact, more than two-thirds of federal workers in the 1992 survey did not have enough information about where to report misconduct. Nearly three-fourths of the workers said they had only limited knowledge of how the federal whistleblower statute protected them from reprisals (GAO 1992).

The Social and Psychological Profile of Whistleblowers

Are particular types of people more likely to be whistle-blowers than others? Does the likelihood of whistleblowing vary by the worker's gender, educational level, age, occupational position, years of employment within the company, general attitudes, and psychological beliefs? Survey data are analyzed here to assess the social and psychological profile of four types of employees: (1) nonobservers of misconduct, (2) silent observers (those who see misconduct but remain silent), (3) internal whistleblowers (those who report misconduct to persons *within* the company), and (4) external whistleblowers (those who report misconduct to authorities *outside* the company).

Demographic Characteristics

There is much debate about the demographic characteristics of whistleblowers—that is, whether there are differences in the likelihood of whistleblowing according to the employee's gender, age, educational level, marital status, and work experiences. Male employees, for example, are often thought to be more prone to whistleblowing than women because they may be less susceptible to peer pressure and majority opinion and may occupy more advanced positions to observe misconduct (Miceli and Near 1992). Similarly, older employees and those with higher educational attainment may hold positions in which internal whistleblowing is expected, but these employees may also be more vested in the company and therefore less willing to report misconduct because of fear of "rocking the boat" within their organization. Single people may be more likely to take risks by reporting organizational conduct because they may feel that it is easier to recover if things go bad, whereas family pressures on married people may persuade these workers to remain quiet and ignore organizational abuses. Demographic differences between whistleblowers and other employees are summarized in Table 4.3.

Gender.   Based on survey data from more than thirteen thousand federal workers (MSPB 1993), women are slightly underrepresented as both internal and external whistleblowers when compared with their distribution among all employees in the sample. Specifically, women comprised 42 percent of all employees in the federal sample, but they accounted for only 38 percent of the internal whistleblowers and 34 percent of the external whistleblowers. Women are also underrepresented as external whistleblowers in our combined statewide samples of employees (55 percent versus 47 percent of all employees).[1] Men make up a higher proportion of external whistleblowers for various subsets of workers, including federal employees, private sector employees, nurses, auditors, supervisors, and nonsupervisors. In short, men are more likely to be external whistleblowers than women, but the differences are fairly small in absolute magnitude.

Age and Work Experience.   Several conflicting possibilities exist in terms of whether younger and novice employees are more likely to observe misconduct and report it. On the one hand, younger and novice employees may be less

---

1. The combined statewide sample of employees includes the following groups: nurses in Nevada, nonprofit employees in Nevada, business and industry employees in Virginia, and workers in various industries across the country.

TABLE 4.3   Social Characteristics of All Employees,
Nonobservers of Misconduct, Silent Observers, Internal
Whistleblowers, and External Whistleblowers

Characteristic by Employee Group	Federal Employee Sample (MSPB 1993) (%)
% Female	
All employees	42
Nonobservers	43
Silent observers	39
Internal whistleblowers	38
External whistleblowers	34
% Less than 40 years old	
All employees	33
Nonobservers	32
Silent observers	37
Internal whistleblowers	34
External whistleblowers	29
% Supervisors	
All employees	27
Nonobservers	27
Silent observers	22
Internal whistleblowers	29
External whistleblowers	35
% Long-term employees	
All employees	56
Nonobservers	56
Silent observers	58
Internal whistleblowers	54
External whistleblowers	62

(continues)

TABLE 4.3 *(continued)*

% Vested workers	
All employees	15
Nonobservers	16
Silent observers	12
Internal whistleblowers	16
External whistleblowers	20
% College educated	
All employees	61
Nonobservers	61
Silent observers	65
Internal whistleblowers	65
External whistleblowers	66

likely to observe fraud, waste, and abuse because their relatively limited work experience places them on the fringe of organizational activity. However, these employees may be more likely to observe some types of misconduct because they are "in the trenches" and may be more prone to be personally victimized by organizational misconduct. Regarding the likelihood and type of whistleblowing, novice employees may be less likely to "rock the boat" by reporting misconduct either inside or outside the company because they fear being fired. Alternatively, these employees may be less vested in the organization and therefore more willing to expose its abuses.

The "seasoned" or "veteran" employee is more likely to have advanced into a managerial or supervisory position, with greater opportunities to observe a wider variety of misconduct. However, as more vested workers, these employees may also have greater tolerance of abuses and actually view misconduct as "normal" activity not worthy of attention. To save their organization adverse publicity, senior workers may be more likely to report misconduct through internal rather than external channels. In contrast, external whistleblowing by these vested workers may be perceived as the only option to correct organizational misconduct and preserve the company's integrity.

To examine differences in observing misconduct and whistleblowing by age and the worker's experiences, the following comparisons were made: (1) workers under forty years old versus those over forty, (2) supervisors versus lower-ranked workers, and (3) employees with less than four years with the company versus those with four or more years of work experience in the organization.

As revealed by the data in Table 4.3, workers under forty years old account for 33 percent of all federal employees, but they represent 37 percent of the silent observers and only 29 percent of the external whistleblowers. Thus they are slightly overrepresented as silent observers and underrepresented as external whistleblowers. The lower rate of external reporting by younger employees is also found across different groups of workers, including different types of federal employees, workers in each of the three sectors (private, public, and nonprofit), supervisors, and nonsupervisors. Although all workers prefer remaining silent over whistleblowing, a higher proportion of younger than older employees do not report organizational misconduct.

Compared to nonsupervisors, supervisors are more likely to be whistleblowers (especially external whistleblowers) and less likely to be silent observers. Long-term employees are also slightly overrepresented as external whistleblowers. Whether explained by greater disenchantment with organizational practices or some other factor, federal workers with either supervisory experience or a long period of federal employment are more likely to be external whistleblowers.

Employees can be classified according to whether they are "vested" in their organization. Vested employees are defined here as those who occupy supervisory positions *and* have been employed at least four years in their organization. Only a small proportion (15 percent) of federal workers occupy vested positions, but a slightly higher concentration of these workers (20 percent) is found among external whistleblowers. Compared to other employees, vested workers are also less likely to remain silent. Even though the conventional wisdom is that organizations should be most fearful of the actions of "fringe members," the results of the federal survey suggest that company "insiders" are actually the employees who are the most prone to violate corporate norms and report abuses to external sources.

Educational Level. There are few differences in the whistleblowing experiences among federal workers by their educational level, but those employees with a college education are slightly more likely to both observe misconduct and report it. This overrepresentation of college-educated workers among external whistleblowers is also found in our state composite sample and among private industry workers, supervisors, and nonsupervisors. Possible explanations for this pattern are that higher-educated workers

(1) are more aware of their legal rights against retaliation and (2) have employment skills that make them more marketable for other jobs and more immune from retaliatory attacks by the organization.

Marital Status. Although data on marital status are not available in the federal survey, the results of our state composite sample indicate that there are few differences in the whistleblowing experiences between married and unmarried workers. Roughly two-thirds of the sample involves married workers, and similar proportions are found among nonobservers, silent observers, internal whistleblowers, and external whistleblowers.

Religious Beliefs. Employees in the state composite samples who said they were "very religious" were slightly overrepresented as external whistleblowers and underrepresented as silent observers. These data provide some limited support for the common assertion that whistleblowers are persons with strong belief systems.

The Whistleblowing Personality

There has been much speculation, and little hard data, on whether a "whistleblowing personality" exists (Jos, Tompkins, and Hays 1989; Miceli and Near 1992). In other words, do whistleblowers have a unique set of psychological and attitudinal characteristics that distinguish them from other employees? If so, what are these characteristics?

A dominant view of whistleblowers held by academics and other professionals is that whistleblowers are principled individuals with strong moral convictions (Jos, Tomp-kins, and Hays 1989; Glazer and Glazer 1989). From this perspective, whistleblowers are thought to be morally prin-cipled, ethical resisters who hold universal standards of conduct, remain uncompromising in their beliefs, maintain a strong sense of social responsibility, and feel they have a high degree of personal control or efficacy over their own lives. This image is clearly incompatible with the public perception of a whistleblower as the snitch. If whistleblow-ers do, in fact, hold these uncompromising positions, it is easy to see why management often views them as "trouble-makers" or at least "difficult" employees (Jos, Tompkins, and Hays 1989).

In surveys of employees in a variety of work settings, we asked them several questions about their general attitudes and personal characteristics. Employees indicated whether they agreed or disagreed with the following statements:

- "Decisions should be made on the basis of universal rules, not on a case-by-case basis."
- "People should make sacrifices for the greater good."
- "People have a responsibility to prevent harm from being done to others."
- "I'm a person of worth."
- "What happens to me is a matter of luck."

Comparison of their responses across four groups of em-ployees (external whistleblowers, internal whistleblowers, silent observers, and nonobservers) allows for an examina-tion of the accuracy of this presumed "whistleblower per-sonality" (see Table 4.4).

TABLE 4.4 General Attitudes of All Employees, Nonobservers of Misconduct, Silent Observers, Internal Whistleblowers, and External Whistleblowers

General Attitudes by Employee Group	% Agreeing
Decisions should be made on a case-by-case basis rather than based on universal rules	
All employees	71
Nonobservers	73
Silent observers	77
Internal whistleblowers	73
External whistleblowers	63
People should make sacrifices for the greater good	
All employees	81
Nonobservers	83
Silent observers	77
Internal whistleblowers	84
External wistleblowers	80
People have a responsibility to prevent harm to others	
All employees	94
Nonobservers	91
Silent observers	94
Internal whistleblowers	93
External whistleblowers	97
I'm a person of worth	
All employees	98
Nonobservers	99
Silent observers	97
Internal whistleblowers	99
External whistleblowers	98

(continues)

TABLE 4.4 *(continued)*

What happens to me is a matter of luck	
All employees	9
Nonobservers	10
Silent observers	5
Internal whistleblowers	11
External whistleblowers	11

Source: State composite employee sample. This sample consists of the following groups: nurses in Nevada, nonprofit employees in Nevada, business and industry employees in Virginia, and workers in various industries across the country.

When compared on these indicators of moral principles, endorsement of universal standards, and feelings of personal control, there are few major differences between whistleblowers and other employees. Whistleblowers are only slightly more likely than other workers to endorse universal standards, believe in making sacrifices for the greater good, feel that people have a responsibility to prevent harm to others, and think they are persons of worth. External whistleblowers were generally more likely to hold these views than internal whistleblowers, but these differences are rather trivial. Contrary to claims that whistleblowers are more principled and ethical employees, there are no major differences between whistleblowers and nonwhistleblowers on these psychological beliefs.

The lack of strong differences between whistleblowers and other employees on personality and sociodemographic factors is important because it suggests that whistleblowing cannot be adequately explained by reference to the personal characteristics of whistleblowers themselves. In other words, we must look for other factors to account for the likelihood and type of whistleblowing. If the demographic profile and general attitudes don't separate whistleblowers from other employees, what does? The importance of situational and organizational factors in understanding whistleblowing is discussed below.

Situational Factors

Social scientists have proposed elaborate decisionmaking models to help explain the conditions under which employees ultimately decide to blow the whistle (see Miceli and Near 1992). From this perspective, whistleblowers are thought to engage in a rational calculus, reaching a decision to speak out or remain silent after logically weighing the anticipated costs and perceived benefits of alternative courses of action. Interviews with whistleblowers and nonwhistleblowers, however, severely question the accuracy of this rational conception for one simple reason: Most whistleblowers are unaware of the costs and benefits of their action. Nonetheless, research does show that the likelihood of whistleblowing is influenced by a wide variety of situational factors (see Table 4.5). What are these factors?

One important situational element is the nature and severity of the observed misconduct. Unless it involves physical harm to other workers or the public at large, most observers of counterproductive work activities (such as leaving work early or taking unauthorized breaks) will only report these acts inside the company (if at all) because the misconduct lacks sufficient "standing" to warrant external action. Ob-

TABLE 4.5 Situational Factors in Whistleblowing

Situational Factor	*Effect on Whistleblowing*
Type of misconduct	
Severe misconduct	> reporting, > external whistleblowing
Public health	> reporting, > external whistleblowing
Counterproductive work activity	< reporting, < external whistleblowing
Prohibited personnel practice	> reporting, > internal and external whistleblowing
Systemic to organization	> external whistleblowing
Frequent misconduct	> reporting
Anonymity	> reporting, > external whistleblowing
Observer-violator relationship	
Close friends/co-workers	< reporting, > internal whistleblowing
Worker/supervisor	< reporting, > external whistleblowing
Employee's stake in company	< reporting, < external whistleblowing
Observer is a co-offender	< reporting
Observer required to act	> reporting

Note: The symbols ">" and "<" refer to whether the presence of the situational factor increases (>) or decreases (<) the likelihood of reporting and the type of whistleblowing. For example, if the type of misconduct is severe, this situational factor increases the likelihood of its being reported and increases the likelihood of external whistleblowing.

servers and victims of prohibited personnel practices such as race discrimination and sexual harassment, in contrast, usually begin with an internal grievance and seek external action only when internal reporting has proved to be unsuccessful. Other than remaining silent, external whistleblowing may be the only option available for observers of systemic and widespread corporate abuses—speaking out to other company officials about the corporation's corruption is likely to bring swift and severe retaliation.

The analysis of survey data from federal employees provides a clear indication of how the type of wrongdoing influences the likelihood and nature of whistleblowing. Nearly 75 percent of the federal workers who observed acts that posed a danger to public safety were whistleblowers. In contrast, only 40 percent of the employees were whistleblowers among observers of such offenses as property theft, improper use of one's position, and providing inadequate goods or services. When the fraud, waste, or abuse involved more than $100,000, the rate of whistleblowing was 58 percent compared to only 8 percent for less serious misconduct. Whistleblowing was more than eight times more likely to occur for systemic wrongdoing (defined as misconduct involving more than $100,000 that occurs on a frequent basis) than it was for other types of misconduct. External rather than internal whistleblowing was also more common for the most serious offenses. Generally, the more severe and frequent the misconduct, the greater the likelihood that employees will become external whistleblowers.

Another situational factor involves the ability to remain anonymous in reporting misconduct. Most people would prefer anonymous reporting if possible to prevent direct re-

taliation from whistleblowing. Wouldn't you? Unfortunately, in most situations, anonymity is impossible. It is hard
to be anonymous, for example, when you're the only one
who has access to the incriminating information. Even if
many people could snitch and you report misconduct in privacy, there is no guarantee that you will be protected. I have
heard of cases in which a whistleblower went upstairs to the
personnel office to file an anonymous complaint about her
supervisor, made the grievance, and—in the time it took to
walk back to her office—had already received a "pink slip"
from her boss. Although confidential whistleblowers are often exposed, the perception that reporting can be done
anonymously increases the likelihood of whistleblowing.

From the perspective of exposing and controlling organizational misconduct, however, a lingering problem with
anonymous reports is that they often suffer from a "credibility" gap and are often not investigated as thoroughly as
cases in which the whistleblower is identified. Anonymity
is a major problem for legal or other remedial action because the whistleblower is often the primary witness who
has unique information about the wrongdoing. Consequently, company officials and law enforcement personnel
often exert strong pressure on whistleblowers to expose
their identify. These pressures may be the reason why
fewer than ten of the 360 whistleblowers interviewed and
surveyed in this study were able to remain anonymous.
Nonetheless, "Deep Throat" is the perfect example of how
whistleblowing can still be highly effective at exposing corruption even under conditions of anonymity.

Another important situational factor is the relationship between the observer and violator. Acts of misconduct involv-

ing close friends who are co-workers are more likely to be ignored than similar conduct done by rivals and less cherished co-workers. Whether or not misconduct by one's supervisor or higher official is reported, however, probably depends on a host of factors including (1) the observer's perception of the likelihood that reporting will result in corrective action, (2) the particular position in the organizational hierarchy held by the violator, (3) the availability of alternative ways of dealing with the problem (such as writing complaints in suggestion boxes, calling whistleblower hot lines, or getting another job), (4) the level of investment or "stakes" the observer has in the company, and (5) whether the observer may be considered legally liable for failing to act. Although these elements seem especially important in cases of misconduct involving higher-ranking officials, these situational factors are salient for understanding the likelihood of whistleblowing in a variety of contexts.

In both our surveys and interviews, respondents were asked "What was the major factor that compelled or persuaded you to report or not report this violation?" Their answers further reveal some of the situational dynamics in whistleblowing. Here is how a representative group of whistleblowers and silent observers in our study responded to this question:

- "It's just not right to do this to people," said a male internal whistleblower who was the victim of racial discrimination by his supervisor.
- "I felt I had to do it because it continued to be done," said a female external whistleblower who reported fraud in auditing reports.

- "I had to do it to save myself and protect my family," said a male external whistleblower who exposed overbilling of the federal government by a post office supervisor.
- "I believe in fair treatment and not jeopardizing the public," said a male external whistleblower who reported numerous problems in the interstate trucking industry.
- "It angers me when wealthy clients are defrauding the government at everyone's expense—it's not right!" said a female external whistleblower who reported on some clients for tax evasion.
- "I had to clear my name—it's a moral travesty to live life with a label of 'sick' that doesn't apply," said a female external whistleblower who was forced to take psychiatric evaluations because she reported widespread cheating on public school exams.
- "I never thought not to [report it]—we were giving out tainted blood—we were going to kill people—it had to stop," said a female external whistleblower who reported that patients had received "bad blood."
- "I was young and inexperienced," said a female silent observer of an executive director embezzling hospital funds.
- "It was my professional duty, it involved public safety, and I was frustrated with company practices," said a male external whistleblower who exposed fraudulent construction practices.
- "I believe in doing the job properly and that people shouldn't get ripped off," said a male internal

whistleblower who observed that contractors were receiving full pay for substandard and nonexistent work.

- "I couldn't sleep well if I let it go on—it wasn't right to do nothing when I knew about it," said a female external whistleblower who reported the misuse of public funds.
- "It was illegal," said a male external whistleblower who exposed his company for falsifying driving records and inspection records for a commercial trucking company.
- "I had the false sense that misconduct could be handled properly," said a female internal whistleblower who observed fraud and gross negligence in her company.
- "I needed to keep my job," said a male silent observer of a co-worker stealing company goods.
- "Arrogance and lawlessness of the command," said a male external whistleblower who saw his military commander force soldiers to report to duty when they were sick.
- "I was threatened with insubordination and termination which made me even more defiant," said a male internal whistleblower who saw his boss overcharge customers and sell used equipment as new.
- "I was always taught to be honest and didn't see any reason to be otherwise," said a male internal whistleblower who reported falsified grade reports in his school.
- "I was told that if I didn't testify, I could be charged as an accessory," said a female external whistle-

blower who reported sexual molestation at a juvenile service agency.

As reflected in these comments, the primary motivation for whistleblowing was neither total altruism nor total self-interest but rather a combination of both. The often mentioned reason that the whistleblower "had to" report misconduct shows that their actions were guided in many cases by situational factors beyond their control.

Organizational Factors

Because whistleblowing occurs within work organizations, a fundamental question is what organizational characteristics are associated with the highest and lowest risks of whistleblowing. Are some organizational structures more conducive to whistleblowing than others? If so, what are the characteristics of these work settings with higher rates of whistleblowing?

Across different work organizations, rates of whistleblowing vary dramatically. At one extreme, all fourteen of the bookstore employees who observed misconduct remained silent within and outside the company. The second most unlikely environment for whistleblowing was in a university administrative unit, where only 12 percent of the observers reported misconduct to a higher-level supervisor within the university and none of them reported it to outside sources. Employees at the high-security manufacturing firm and petrochemical plants had the next highest rates of whistleblowing. At the other end, auditors and nurses as occupational groups were the most likely whistleblowers; more than 80 percent of the auditors and more than 50 percent of the nurses reported misconduct to someone within or outside their workplace. Almost one out of four auditors who were whistleblowers reported it to external sources compared to less than 10 percent among nurses.

Among federal employees, about 50 percent of the observers of fraud, waste, or abuse were whistleblowers regardless of the type of work they did. However, external whistleblowing for federal employees was most common among those employed in the legal field (54 percent), whereas less than 20 percent of the federal whistleblowers in clerical positions or the fields of science or engineering made external disclosures.

What is it about work organizations and occupational roles that accounts for the wide variability in whistleblowing?

The high rate of whistleblowing among external auditors and nurses is explained by the occupational roles and expectations for each type of employee. Take first external auditors. These employees are guided by a professional code of ethics and strong organizational policies within auditing firms concerning the appropriate means of reporting misconduct. Recent federal legislation has been enacted that makes external auditors legally obligated to report fraud and misconduct to government officials. Given this climate for reporting misconduct within auditing firms, it should not be surprising that external auditors feel relatively more comfortable than other employees in reporting observed misconduct to other company officials. Their high rate of external whistleblowing is probably related to this code of ethics, the belief that whistleblowing is role-prescribed behavior, a growing moral or legal responsibility on auditors to disclose misconduct (stemming from incidents like the savings and loan scandal), and changes in federal law regulating their official conduct.

The high prevalence of whistleblowing among nurses is also explained by their organizational role. Specifically, their role as double agents in the medical field—that is, serving the patient and the hospital—places nurses in a position in which internal whistleblowing may be functional for both groups. By disclosing medical incompetence or maltreatment to hospital officials, the nurse protects the patient from further harm and saves the hospital from negative publicity and major lawsuits. However, work organizations often send rather mixed messages about the appropriateness of whistleblowing that subsequently limit its extent. In the case of nurses, the major impediment to external whistleblowing (and even internal reporting) is that it violates the sacred trust between nurses and doctors. The threat of retaliation for violating this trust also limits the level of whistleblowing even among these public servants.

The characteristics of the organization and individuals' occupational roles also account for the level of whistleblowing in other organizations. In the case of the bookstore employees, fear of losing their jobs for snitching and the inability to find alternative employment in a rural area were the primary motivations for remaining silent. The majority of employees at the high-security plant and petrochemical company were unwilling to be whistleblowers because of similar economic conditions and the relatively high pay for employment in these companies for unskilled and semiskilled laborers. However, in the high-security facility, there is an added incentive for whistleblowing on particular types of misconduct: Failing to report some violations may result in serious injury and death to many co-workers. These crosscurrents help explain the higher rate of whistleblowing in the high-security environment than in the petrochemical plant of comparable size.

Across all organizational settings and particular jobs within organizations, external whistleblowing is clearly the exception rather than the rule. The only group of employees that had a higher rate of external than internal whistleblowing was federal workers in the legal field. For all other groups of federal and nonfederal employees, less than 30 percent of the whistleblowers reported misconduct to outside sources. These findings are explained by societal norms against "airing dirty laundry" and the strong pressures exerted by management to deal with organizational deviance "in house." Given that public exposure of organizational misconduct may have major financial consequences, management will go to extraordinary lengths to keep misconduct out of public view. This includes the recruitment of new employees who fit the organization's mission and do not "rock the boat." Through the professional socialization of "like-minded" recruits, organizational values of silence are reinforced and the possibility of attacks from within by disloyal employees is minimized.

Another possible explanation for the low rate of external whistleblowing involves the effectiveness of management's response to internal complaints. Specifically, our interviews strongly support the findings in previous research that external reporting usually occurs after internal channels have proven ineffective (Miethe and Rothschild 1994). When management is considered inert or duplicitous in the wrongdoing, external reporting may be the only option for whistleblowers. By being responsive to the initial complaint and taking corrective action to prevent further wrongdoing, managers in the organizations studied here may have thwarted the necessity of external whistleblowing.

Previous studies indicate that several additional organizational factors influence the likelihood and type of whistleblowing. These factors include the organization's values, hierarchical structure, and complexity.

As you may have noticed at your place of work, the values held by management, but especially those of the CEO, set the moral or ethical tone for the entire organization. If the CEO is considered a buffoon, tyrant, or egomaniac who lacks basic human values, both productivity and worker allegiance to the company are likely to diminish. Why work hard or care about your company when you detest the big boss? Employees have been known to sabotage work just to make life miserable for employers they do not respect. In these work environments, employees who observe misconduct are probably not going to waste their time by reporting it up the chain of command. Instead, external whistleblowing provides an excellent opportunity to expose incompetent management and dilute their power. Supporting this view, only 28 percent of the external whistleblowers in our study thought their employer had strong moral values, compared to more than 50 percent of the silent observers and internal whistleblowers who held similar attitudes toward their boss.

A different story exists in work organizations in which the CEO is considered fair and of high integrity. Employees in these settings may work harder to resolve problems in a less threatening informal manner and feel at greater ease talking to management about misconduct without fear of reprisals. Such executives also provide a variety of ways for employees to voice their concerns, including suggestion boxes, weekly open meetings, and office hot lines for the anonymous reporting of misconduct. When senior management is responsive to the concerns of workers and takes immediate corrective action to deal with misconduct, there is no need for external whistleblowing.

Another important organizational characteristic is the complexity of the bureaucratic structure. Previous research suggests that small, less formalized, less bureaucratic, and more participatory work environments may have higher rates of internal whistleblowing (and less external reporting) because there is more group solidarity, there are more entrenched norms of trust and openness in working relationships, and there is greater personal investment in organizational success (Miethe and Rothschild 1994). Within more formalized and bureaucratic organizations, employees may feel that their company is more rule-bound and less responsive to internal complaints. Our interviews with workers also support this characterization. Specifically, twice as many internal whistleblowers as external whistleblowers believed that their company had a democratic decisionmaking process and opportunities for employee input. Put a different way, external whistleblowers often come from work environments that are considered rigid, bureaucratic, and nonresponsive to employees' concerns.

Summary

This chapter examined the extent of whistleblowing and identified some of the personal, situational, and organizational causes of whistleblowing. Remaining silent is the typical response when employees observe misconduct at work. Of the two types of whistleblowing, internal reporting is far more common than external disclosure.

Contrary to the claims of other researchers, there is little evidence of a "whistleblowing personality." A person's age, gender, educational attainment, religiosity, and position within the company say little about who will blow the whistle and who will not. Attitudes indicative of one's endorsement of universal standards of conduct, social responsibility, and feelings of self-control are not necessarily more common among whistleblowers than other employees. Whistleblowing, however, is strongly influenced by a host of situational and organizational factors. The nature and severity of the original misconduct, the opportunity for anonymous reporting, the availability of alternative ways of dealing with the problem, the interpersonal relationship between the observer and violator, one's occupational role, perceptions of the organization's values or culture, and the organization's structure are important determinants of the likelihood and type of whistleblowing.

5

Individual and Organizational Consequences of Whistleblowing

Very few whistleblowers either understand or anticipate the consequences of their action. Regardless of whether one is an internal or external whistleblower, there are both costs and benefits for speaking out against organizational misconduct. The personal and societal consequences of whistleblowing are described below.

The Personal Benefits

Although often overlooked (because we tend to focus on the negative side of snitching), there are numerous and diverse personal benefits from whistleblowing. Personal benefits have both social and financial dimensions.

One immediate personal benefit of whistleblowing involves feelings of self-efficacy and personal gratification. Americans often feel a lack of control over their lives, being acted upon rather than acting. Snitching and whistleblowing, however, provide a means of gaining control. By disclosing inside knowledge, whistleblowers are essentially telling others of their privileged status as insiders and may reap some personal gratification from being able to act like the proverbial "big wig." Whistleblowing for these people serves as a means of self-enhancement.

Whistleblowing may also be personally gratifying for other reasons. Self-satisfaction may stem from exposing some wrongdoing, preventing a greater harm, or "burning" someone you don't like. There may be a great deal of personal pride in exposing mass corruption (at great personal risks) and playing a major role in preventing harm to others. Less glorious, but equally gratifying to some, snitching can make a rival's life miserable. If our personality and sense of self are formed by the feedback we receive from others, whistleblowing on serious corporate or political abuses (as done by "Deep Throat," Frank Serpico, Karen Silkwood, and Jeffrey Wigand in the tobacco industry) may contribute to the development of a positive self-image. Ironically, the struggles that face most whistleblowers may also have positive consequences or benefits: Those struggles may increase the whistleblowers' awareness of how to expose violations in more constructive ways in the future.

Over the last two decades, the use of perks for snitching has become largely institutionalized in our society. Employees are told to call this "tipster" number or "Secret Witness" and get a reward for snitching or to become a paid informant and receive financial compensation for relocation. The "rat" receives a reassignment to a less strenuous job, special visitor passes, or a pack of smokes. The same thing applies to whistleblowers. For these snitches, however, compensation may involve a year-end bonus, a well-deserved day off, or small cash award.

Under the False Claims Act, whistleblowers can receive up to 30 percent of the recovered costs from persons and organizations who defraud the federal government. The number of these cases filed nationally has risen dramatically over the last decade, increasing from thirty-three cases in 1987 to 274 cases in 1995 (Phillips and Cohen 1996). The total fraud recovery under the False Claims Act exceeded $1 billion over that time period. The following list of the most lucrative government recoveries and financial awards that went to individual whistleblowers from lawsuits under the False Claims Act is taken from materials published by Taxpayers Against Fraud (TAF 1995, 1996, 1997a):

- $182 million was recovered from Laboratory Corporation of America Holdings for false claims involving medically unnecessary "add-on" tests submitted to Medicare, Medicaid, and the Civilian Health and Medical Program of the Uniform Services (CHAMPUS). The financial awards for the whistleblowers included $625,000 to Geoffrey Zuccolo and $338,000 to Mary Downy. Shares of an unknown dollar amount were also awarded to two other whistleblowers in this case.
- United Technologies Corporation (UTC) agreed to pay $150 million to settle a lawsuit alleging that its Sikorsky Aircraft Division prematurely billed for work not yet performed on its helicopter contract with the U.S. military. The suit also alleged that UTC attempted

to suppress disclosure of the improper practices. The whistleblower received $22.5 million for his actions.

- $88 million was recovered from Lucas Western Inc. and Lucas Industries for false tests of military components, defective parts, and falsification of inspections. Frederick Copeland received nearly $18.5 million for disclosing these violations.

- $84 million was recovered from Damon Clinical Laboratories for fraudulent billing of Medicare, Medicaid, and CHAMPUS. Jeanne Bryne received $9 million, and $1.5 million was awarded to Jack Dowden and Kevin Spear for reporting these medical fraud practices.

- $27.6 million was recovered from Blue Cross Blue Shield of Michigan for improper billing and submitting false documentation as fiscal intermediary for Medicare and for inadequate audits of hospital cost reports. Darcy Flynn received $5.5 million for her whistleblowing actions.

- $13 million was recovered from FMC Corporation for inflating military contracts including amounts for independent research and development and for bid and proposal projects. Robert Neargarter received $2.86 million for reporting these violations.

- $12 million was recovered from Accudyne Corporation and Alliant TechSystems, Inc., for nonconforming military components and the failure to properly test them and for noncompliance with environmental requirements. Several individual whistleblowers and the Atlantic States Legal Foundation received $2.64 million for their disclosures.

- $11 million was recovered from Corning Clinical Laboratories Inc. and Unilab Corporation (MetPath Inc.) for false billing of Medicare, Medicaid, and CHAMPUS for blood indices not ordered or medically necessary. Kevin Spear and Jack Dowden received $1.6 million for their whistleblowing actions. In a separate legal action against MetPath Inc., Terry Fletcher received $1.29 million of an $8.6 million settlement against the company for submitting false claims for laboratory tests that were not performed.
- $7.2 million was recovered from General Electric Company for the failure to satisfy electrical bonding requirements for aircraft engines. Ian Johnson received $1.7 million for his disclosures.

These financial rewards are impressive, but they are clearly the exception rather than the rule. As described in Chapter 6, there are also major eligibility restrictions that limit both the actual opportunity and the amount of the award for whistleblowers in these lawsuits. Nonetheless, for a few select whistleblowers, the False Claims Act provides an opportunity for large financial benefits for reporting fraudulent practices against government programs or contracts.

The Personal Costs

The personal costs for reporting organizational and occupational misconduct vary in their type and magnitude. Actual reprisals or threats of retaliation by management for whistleblowing include informal actions (shunning the worker or verbal harassment), formal reprimands (firing and demo-tions), and extra-organizational measures (blacklisting work-ers from future employment and physical attacks against them or family members). For whistleblowers who remain in the organization, there is often a loss of personal autonomy and greater surveillance of their work activities. Retaliation by co-workers may involve shunning the whistleblowers, verbal harassment, physical intimidation, or the sabotage of their work. Interpersonally, whistleblowing often strains family relations and friendship networks. Deteriorating mental and physical health, psychological and financial stress, depression, growing distrust and a sense of alienation, and substance or alcohol abuse are some of the behavioral consequences for the individual whistleblower.

Organizational retaliation can take various forms, some blatant and some less obvious. Depending upon what the misconduct is and how it is reported, the organization may go to extraordinary lengths to silence and discredit whistle-blowers. Some of the methods used against whistleblowers by organizations have included building a damaging record against them, threatening and isolating them, pub-licly humiliating them, reassigning them to the most dan-gerous job settings, sabotaging their careers through nega-tive reference letters for future employment, having them prosecuted for theft of evidentiary documents, providing them tasks that are designed to fail, denying them access to resources, extraditing those who are foreign nationals, and placing gag orders in contracts and then pressing legal ac-tion for their violation (GAP 1997b).

National survey data from federal employees in 1992 provide estimates of the prevalence of different types of organizational and interpersonal retaliation against whistle-blowers (see MSPB 1993). Among the nearly fifteen hundred federal survey respondents who observed and reported misconduct within the preceding twelve months, the proportion of identified whistleblowers exposed to each type of retaliation (in decreasing prevalence) included:

- 23 percent, verbal harassment or intimidation
- 22 percent, poor performance appraisal
- 20 percent, shunned by co-workers or managers
- 18 percent, assignment to less desirable or less important duties
- 13 percent, denial of award
- 11 percent, denial of promotion
- 10 percent, transfer or reassignment to a different job with less desirable duties
- 9 percent, denial of opportunity for training
- 3 percent, reassignment to a different geographical location
- 3 percent, suspension from the job
- 2 percent, grade level demotion
- 2 percent, required to take a fitness-for-duty exam
- 1 percent, fired from the job

It is important to recognize that these estimates of retaliation are conservative and undercount the prevalence of reprisals for whistleblowing. This is the case because much organizational retaliation is hidden and unknown to the whistleblower. Under these conditions, termination or reassignment due to "reduction in force" and other legitimate bases for changes in employment status may serve as convenient institutional outlets for retaliation against whistle-blowers.

Comparisons of federal data over time reveal several trends about changes in the nature and type of retaliation. First, rates of retaliation against federal workers have increased over time. Thirty-seven percent of federal workers in 1992 who reported some type of illegal or wasteful activity thought they were threatened or had experienced some type of reprisal, compared to only 24 percent of whistleblowers in the 1983 federal survey. This increase is surprising when one considers the dramatic growth in the availability of whistleblowing protection through various federal and state statutes during this same time period. Second, changes over time in reprisals against whistle-blowers vary by the specific type of alleged retaliation. Most official personnel actions (such as demotions, firings, and suspensions), for example, have shown a distinct decline since the 1983 survey (MSPB 1993). However, another type of personnel action, poor performance evaluations, was directly experienced by 21 percent of the whistleblow-ers in 1983 but had at least doubled in frequency to 47 percent in 1992.

Rates of retaliation are far higher among respondents in our state composite sample of employees across a variety of work settings. For example, more than two-thirds of these whistleblowers had experienced at least one of the following types of reprisals:

- lost their job or were forced to retire
- received negative job performance evaluations
- work was more closely monitored by supervisors

- criticized and ignored by co-workers
- blacklisted by the company

The estimates of retaliation against whistleblowing derived both from our research and the MSPB federal surveys, however, are probably distorted because of inherent problems with each data source. The federal surveys undercount the level of retaliation because they omit workers who have been fired or have quit federal employment because of their whistleblowing experience. Our survey results probably overestimate the frequency of retaliation because these respondents have gone farther to seek relief by eliciting outside assistance or information (by contacting me directly or by contacting Integrity International, Dr. Soeken's support group for whistleblowers). Both data sources undercount the prevalence of hidden forms of retaliation. Owing to the conflicting sources of survey bias, a reasonable estimate of the proportion of all whistleblowers in the United States who experience reprisals lies between these two sources. Under this assumption, about half of all whistleblowers are expected to experience severe retaliation by management for their disclosures.

Our survey of employees in a variety of work settings provides the only available estimates of other interpersonal and behavioral consequences of whistleblowing. Serious reductions in the quality of life are a common consequence of whistleblowing. For example, more than two-thirds of whistleblowers felt that their physical health, mental health, and financial situation had all worsened after reporting the misconduct. Severe depression and anxiety, feelings of isolation and powerlessness, and distrust of others were experienced by more than 80 percent of whistle-blowers. Their disclosures ultimately resulted in financial bankruptcy for about half of them.

For many whistleblowers, the process of reporting misconduct and the subsequent reprisals for their action result in a dramatic transformation of their personal identities. Specifically, the label "whistleblower" becomes one's "master status" that influences and alters all other aspects of life.

As applied by sociologists and social psychologists, the master status is the primary element of one's personal identity (see Hughes 1945; Miethe and McCorkle 1997). A person's race, gender, age, and physical stature are all major status characteristics that have been considered "master" statuses in a variety of contexts. Given a specific trait (for instance, being a "senior citizen"), secondary traits are also assumed (such as diminished physical/mental abilities and sex dysfunction) that become part of one's personal identity. In a similar vein, the act of whistleblowing and its consequences become a master status that totally engulfs and overrides other aspects of one's life. The struggle in exposing misconduct becomes, in many cases, a lifelong campaign to clear one's name and reputation. In other cases, the obsession over the events and the frequent rehashing of them begin to wear thin on family and friends, ultimately resulting in the disengagement of the whistleblower from these supporters. The loss of co-workers, friends, and family members fuels the anger and feelings of victimization that often characterize whistleblowing. The whistleblower who survives the experience and is unscathed in the process is the rare exception.

Personal and Situational Correlates
of Retaliation

The nature and magnitude of organizational and individual retaliation against whistleblowers vary across individual workers and situational contexts. Some employees may experience swift and severe retaliation for reporting misconduct, whereas others are insulated from it. Similarly, some types of reporting may be expected behavior in some organizational contexts, whereas the same reporting practices may be severely condemned in other settings. Several of these personal and situational correlates of the nature and likelihood of retaliation against whistleblowers are summarized below.

Personal Characteristics

There are some demographic differences among whistleblowers in their likelihood of experiencing retaliation. Federal workers in supervisory positions and those supervisors employed in their current job for more than four years are far less likely than nonsupervisors and relatively new employees to face reprisals for whistleblowing. The greater insulation of these vested employees from reprisals is explained by their more privileged position within the organization. There are no differences according to the whistleblower's gender, age, or educational attainment in their risks of reprisals. African American employees, however, were nearly twice as likely as white employees to experience retaliation for whistleblowing.

Type of Whistleblowing

One of the major situational factors that dramatically influences the likelihood of retaliation is the type of whistleblowing. Internal whistleblowing is far less likely to elicit retaliation than is external whistleblowing to persons outside the company. Among federal workers, external whistleblowers are nearly 10 percentage points more likely to experience any reprisals (31 percent versus 22 percent) and severe reprisals such as demotions, suspensions, and termination (26 percent versus 17 percent) than internal whistleblowers. Although external whistleblowers may gain some protection or immunity by going public with their allegations, the higher likelihood of organizational retaliation against them is the result of their violation of the sacred rule of keeping things "in house."

Type of Misconduct

The likelihood of retaliation for whistleblowing on individual and organizational misconduct also depends on the nature and gravity of the initial violation. Disclosure of rare and trivial misconduct by co-workers or junior management may result in personal retaliation by these employees, but it rarely elicits reprisals by the larger organization unless the violator is a valued member within the company. In contrast, the external reporting of frequent and serious misconduct that is systemic to the operation and the success of the organization is likely to result in quick and severe reprisals.

Data on federal workers collected by the Merit System Protection Board confirm the relationships between the seriousness of misconduct, its frequency, and the likelihood of reprisals. The reporting of illegal and unethical practices that occur frequently is three times more likely to elicit retaliation than activities that occur once or rarely. The disclosure of activities that involved more than $100,000 was more than twice as likely to result in retaliation as activities with a value of less than $100. Almost half of the whistleblowers who reported both frequent and serious misconduct to external agents experienced reprisals for their actions. Even though federal workers have legal protection against retaliation, more than one-third of the external whistleblowers suffered serious organizational reprisals.

The most widely publicized cases of whistleblowing are notorious because of the nature and magnitude of organizational misconduct and the subsequent severity of the retaliation against the whistleblower. The shooting of Frank Serpico, after his allegations of corruption in the New York Police Department, and Karen Silkwood's suspicious death in an automobile accident, after reporting safety violations in the nuclear industry, are examples of these high-profile whistleblowers whose sagas have been told on the big screen. Several of the whistleblowers we have interviewed have also experienced physical injury and death threats for their disclosures of major violations. However, the typical whistleblower's allegations and subsequent retaliation are no less real, but usually far less dramatic, than these high-profile cases.

Anonymous Reporting

Anonymous reporting, although having less impact on changing organizational practices, obviously provides greater protection against retaliation. However, being able to report misconduct anonymously and remaining anonymous are often quite different things. Most organizations have some mechanism for anonymous reporting (a personnel office or hot lines), but anonymity is often illusive because only a few people have the opportunity to detect and observe many forms of organizational misconduct. Nonetheless, the ability to conceal one's identity is a major safeguard against reprisals. Among federal workers, 36 percent of whistleblowers whose identity was known to the violator experienced retaliation compared to only 10 percent of the anonymous whistleblowers. This latter finding suggests that even remaining anonymous does not absolutely guarantee the whistleblower's safety from attacks by co-workers and management.

Organizational Climate

Like the findings that some organizations are more prone to whistleblowing than others, it is also the case that organizations vary in their likelihood of retaliation. Even though little data exist to evaluate these claims, it makes sense that private, profit-motivated businesses would be more prone both to organizational misconduct (because profit margins in the private sector often hinge on the ability to operate on the margins between legitimate and illegitimate business practices) and to retaliation against whistleblowers (because the businesses have more to lose by the disclosures). As will be discussed in Chapter 6, workers in private businesses also have less protection and legal recourse from "at will" termination and other types of retaliation.

Regardless of the type of industry or business, the low tolerance of some organizations for individual and organizational misconduct creates a climate in which whistleblowers are encouraged to disclose abuses and offered protection against reprisals. The CEO often sets the moral or ethical tone for the entire organization (Clinard 1983). Corporations like IBM, Boeing, Harley Davidson, and Home Depot are often considered the most progressive and worker-friendly companies that have good track records for dealing with individual and organizational misconduct. It isn't surprising in these work environments that retaliation is a less common response for reporting illegal and unethical behavior.

The Collective Benefits of Whistleblowing

Although often downplayed in the popular press and everyday conversations, whistleblowing has several collective benefits for organizations and the wider society. These involve the social and economic benefits of eliminating and controlling individual and organizational misconduct.

As employees or former employees, whistleblowers are in a unique position to observe misconduct in work organizations. They work within the environment and, in many cases, have the necessary access to financial records and documents to detect misconduct. Such external agents as inspectors and auditors are not able to monitor ongoing organizational practices nearly as well as employees themselves. Monitoring actions by fellow employees is also less likely to raise suspicion by company employees engaging in the criminal or unethical activity. Under these conditions, employees are clearly in the best position to observe and report organizational misconduct.

From the perspective of the wider society, the most obvious benefit of whistleblowing is its potential for reporting and subsequently deterring organizational misconduct. The enormous economic costs that are ultimately passed on to the public for such offenses as employee theft, corporate tax fraud, misappropriation of funds, consumer fraud, and other types of occupational and organizational crime may be greatly reduced by the threat of detection provided by employees as potential whistleblowers.

One indication of the economic benefits from whistleblowing is the amount of financial losses recovered through fraud hot lines. Employee hot lines for reporting various types of fraud, waste, and abuse have been developed across many federal and state agencies. In fact, there are at least forty-six separate federal departments and agencies with hot lines for reporting fraud, waste, and abuse (GAO 1988a). Two of the most widely known hot lines include:

- The U.S. Department of Defense (DOD) hot line for reporting potential wrongdoing or mismanagement in the military. During its first six years of operation, there were more than 28,000 telephone and letter contacts to the DOD hot line, resulting in substantiated allegations in 15,500 cases (GAO 1988a). The total financial savings from DOD hot line activities average nearly $15 million per year.
- The General Accounting Office (GAO) fraud hot line was established to allow anyone to report allegations of fraud or mismanagement of federal funds. During

its first ten years, more than 94,000 calls were made to the GAO hot line, involving about 14,000 substantiated referrals of misconduct to other agencies (GAO 1988a).

As a channel for whistleblowing, the anonymity associated with hot line reporting provides the worker with greater protection against retaliation. In addition, persons who use these hot lines probably would not be willing to report misconduct directly to agency personnel or outside authorities. Under these conditions, society clearly benefits from this type of whistleblowing through the unique opportunities that hot lines provide for exposing fraud, waste, and abuse in government and industry.

Organizations that experience fraud, waste, and abuse may also benefit directly from whistleblowers in several respects. First, disclosures by co-workers of illegal and unethical conduct allow organizations to identify "bad apples" within their company. By identifying problem employees early, whistleblowers may thwart the development of more serious misconduct in the company. Second, internal whistleblowing may save the offending organization widespread adverse publicity and economic backlash. If reported early and dealt with swiftly within the company, the potential disruption caused by the original misconduct is minimized. For example, the great loss in charitable contributions to United Way after the disclosure of the extravagant lifestyle of the ex-CEO and the scathing publicity surrounding the Tail-Hook military scandals may have been minimized by timely reports by fellow officials and subsequent corrective action within these organizations.

As a strategy for changing organizational practices, however, it is important to note that whistleblowing is only an effective control measure under particular conditions. Not all people are equally effective as whistleblowers, and even the most important whistleblower traits may be rendered impotent in particular work environments. For instance, the following characteristics are often thought to be associated with successful whistleblowing: external reporting, being in a supervisory position, having extensive documentation of the offense, and persistence. However, none of these characteristics will necessarily result in changes in organizational practices if (1) the violation occurs in a state and industry that offer no legal protection to employees against retaliatory discharge or (2) the offending organization has almost total monopolistic control over the distribution or production of a particular good or service in the marketplace. Nonetheless, although the disclosure of any particular act may not result in immediate constructive change in individual and organizational practices, whistleblowing has enormous potential as a tool for improving the public good.

The Collective Costs of Whistleblowing

Regardless of its benefits to organizations and the wider society, there are several major costs of whistleblowing as a form of social control in the modern workplace. The primary costs of whistleblowing include its use as a source of slander and organizational sabotage and its promotion of greater surveillance and lower worker autonomy.

There is no doubt that whistleblowing for some employees provides a rather nefarious means of personal slander and organizational sabotage. Claims of gross misconduct, no matter their truth, may result in irreversible harm. Supervisors and managers charged with sexual harassment, for example, may suffer unwarranted reprimands from their employer or experience interpersonal hardships (for instance, loss of co-worker loyalty/friendship or marital conflict) solely based on these allegations. Similar trauma often characterizes criminal defendants who are falsely accused and subsequently acquitted of wrongdoing. Persons found innocent under these circumstances are commonly viewed as guilty people who are beating the rap.

For organizations falsely accused of wrongdoing by whistleblowers, the consequences of these allegations may include loss of public confidence and even financial disaster. The power of adverse publicity is clearly revealed in several recent cases. Publicity surrounding the deaths and illnesses from the *Escherichia coli* (more commonly known as *E. coli*) bacteria of persons who ate undercooked hamburgers at Jack-in-the-Box restaurants had a dramatic impact on their profits. Allegations of racial discrimination in employment practices by Texaco and the subsequent boycott promoted by the Reverend Jesse Jackson are other instances of the power of adverse publicity. For organizations that rely upon public trust and do not have a monopoly over the market, fabricated allegations by disgruntled employees may cause the financial ruin of the organization. Later admonishments against the whistleblower for inaccurate disclosures do little good in repairing the harm.

The frequency of use of whistleblowing as a means of defaming co-workers and sabotaging the organization, however, is limited by several factors. First, most large companies have someone in the capacity of an ombudsperson or reporting/hearing officer who reviews and investigates cases of potential fraud, waste, and abuse. Any outrageous claims of individual or organizational misconduct could be effectively silenced and discredited at this early stage. Second, most reputable journalists and other outside reporting agents require some factual evidence of misconduct to corroborate another's allegations. Without this confirmation, whistleblowers' allegations are going to have little credibility. Third, the threat of legal action against the whistleblower for slander or defamation of character serves as a possible deterrent for unfounded allegations. Under these conditions, whistleblowing may have great potential as a means for personal and institutional sabotage, but there are several safeguards that limit the prevalence of using whistleblowing solely for these purposes.

Another major societal cost of whistleblowing involves the greater surveillance of workers and the loss of worker autonomy. The Orwellian notion that "big brother" is watching has become an increasingly common reality in modern society. The dramatic rise in surveillance technology has made all types of monitoring far more prevalent. Time and motion technologies monitor the productivity levels of industrial workers. Video surveillance equipment has expanded from primarily banking and financial institutions to convenience stores, movie theaters, apartment complexes, and even highways to catch speeders and stoplight violators. Parents use video and audio systems to monitor their babies in bed, and suspicious persons can purchase relatively inexpensive "spy kits" to track the activities of lovers and spouses.

Within this wider context of surveillance, the ability of employees to easily report misconduct by co-workers and the possibility of receiving social and financial rewards for doing so ultimately create a predatory environment that diminishes worker autonomy and the quality of work life. When any slipup may result in an action report by co-workers and a reprimand by the company, two negative outcomes are likely to happen. First, employees will become more alienated and disenchanted because their sense of autonomy at work and friendship ties with co-workers will be severely threatened by the greater surveillance. Second, both productivity and innovation in these work environments are likely to diminish because employees will be overly cautious in production activities and not willing to take chances and try alternatives, owing to fear of reprisals. Of course, the positive side of whistleblowing is that it does serve as a potential deterrent for illegal and unethical activity in the modern workplace (see Miethe and Rothschild 1994). Depending upon the frequency and gravity of the wrongdoing, the positive benefits from whistleblowing in exposing and deterring misconduct may be greater or far less than the costs in worker autonomy and co-worker loyalty that are likely consequences of the whistleblowing.

Summary

Whistleblowing is associated with both individual and organizational costs and benefits. The primary costs to the individual whistleblower involve various types of retaliation. Whistleblowers may obtain some personal benefits from disclosing misconduct in the face of adversity. Organizations benefit from internal whistleblowing because it helps identify bad employees and thwarts the development of more widespread and serious misconduct. Whistleblowing's major cost to the organization is its impact on declining public trust, and subsequent financial resources, upon the exposure of the fraud, waste, or abusive practices. The wider society benefits from whistleblowing through the disclosure and ultimate control of organizational misconduct, whereas the major cost of whistleblowing lies in the promotion of greater surveillance and reductions in workers' autonomy.

6

The Legal Protection of Whistleblowers

Legal protection for individuals has been increasingly extended since the 1960s to nearly all aspects of social life, and whistleblowing is no exception. A wide range of laws now protect federal employees from retaliatory discharge in a variety of work settings. Legislative statutes in many states offer protection to employees in the public sector, and similar protection is provided to workers in private business in some states. Judicial rulings that make up the evolving states' common law about "at-will" terminations also provide the basis for legal action against unlawful employment practices. Administrative rules and codes of ethics in some professions are other forums for the protection of employees.

Knowing your legal rights and the particular activities that are legally protected is essential for becoming a successful whistleblower. Unfortunately, an accurate determination of what constitutes a protected activity and wrongful discharge is often difficult to predict, is usually written in a language not understandable by nonlawyers, and varies dramatically across different types of employees and state boundaries.

Numerous technicalities about jurisdiction, legal standing, and statutes of limitations often preempt whistleblowers' attempts to receive legal protection for their actions.

The legal protections for whistleblowers are reviewed in this chapter, beginning with a review of the different domains of legal protection and descriptions of exceptions to the "at-will" termination doctrine that derive from common law, federal statutory protections, and state statutes. *Qui tam* lawsuits under the False Claims Act are discussed as a particular legal approach that offers potentially large rewards for disclosing particular types of misconduct. The chapter concludes with an evaluation of the overall effectiveness of current legal remedies for whistleblowers.

Factors Influencing Legal Protection

There is no universal standard or legal rule that provides uniform protection for all whistleblowers. Instead, the specific legal protection afforded a particular whistleblower depends on a variety of factors. For employees who blow the whistle, a combination of federal and state statutes, judicial rulings, and administrative regulations defines (1) *who* is protected from wrongful discharge, (2) *what* types of misconduct and reprisals for reporting it are covered, (3) *when* legal protection begins and whether there is a statute of limitations for filing legal action, (4) the jurisdictions *where* workers are most protected from wrongful discharge, and (5) *how* employees should proceed with a formal complaint.

An initial determinant of the level and nature of whistleblowing protection involves whether the worker is employed in the public or private sector. Persons employed in the public sector (such as public school teachers and employees of federal/state/local government and its agencies) are provided a wider array of legal protection than workers in private industries. Most public employees are covered through various federal and state legislation as well as judicially derived exceptions to the at-will termination doctrine. Private employees are equally protected by the evolving common law on at-will terminations but are given statutory protection in only a few states.

The availability and nature of whistleblower protection also vary by the type of alleged misconduct. For example, unlawful discharge for reporting violations of one type of federal law (for instance, the Clean Air Act) offers particular remedies and special conditions that may be quite different from other federal statutes. Even within the same type of violation (such as toxic waste disposal), state and federal statutory protections may vary dramatically in their coverage, remedies, and special conditions. Some state and federal laws also specify that the alleged misconduct must be substantial (e.g., including such terminology as "gross waste of funds" and "substantial and specific danger to public health"), whereas other statutes do not place restrictions on the gravity of alleged misconduct.

Whether one's disclosures of a prohibited personnel practice, fraud, waste, or other abuses are protected also depends on how the whistleblowing is done. Legal protection is provided for wrongful discharge for internal disclosures of misconduct in some federal and state statutes but not in others (Kohn and Kohn 1988). Some states require employees to report violations first to their supervisors; protection is not provided for employees who violate this sequence by reporting misconduct initially to external agents. Conversely, some federal workers (for instance, those at nuclear power plants) can be denied protection from wrongful discharge under a particular federal statute if they report their violation initially to their supervisor rather than to an external regulatory agency (Kohn and Kohn 1988).

It is unreasonable to think that any employee would be totally aware of his or her legal protection across these various situational factors. The determination of what constitutes unlawful discharge of whistleblowers becomes even more complex when the full array of legislative and judicial protection is considered.

Types of Legal Protection

Whistleblower protection against unlawful discharge and other types of retaliation is provided primarily through three different forums: (1) exceptions to the at-will termination doctrine derived from judicially based common law, (2) federal statutes, and (3) state statutes. Over the past two decades, a growing number of whistleblowers have used civil remedies through the False Claims Act to receive large monetary awards for exposing fraudulent practices against the government. The nature and scope of each of these developments are described below.

The Termination At-Will Doctrine

Most workers throughout U.S. history have labored under conditions of limited job security and protection. Up until the early twentieth century, employees were hired and fired "at will" by their employers. Except those given assurances through private contracts, employees during that time period essentially had no legal rights. Workers hired for an indefinite time period could be terminated for any reason (or "no reason" at all), and their employers could use this power to compel them to work at no minimum wage, no maximum hours, and in dangerous and hazardous working conditions (Kohn and Kohn 1988). Employers had similar discretion to hire without question whomever they wanted. Allegations of discriminatory hiring or firing practices based on the employee's sex, race, or other status characteristics had no legal standing.

The doctrine of employment at-will has eroded over time as an increasing number of exceptions to this doctrine have been judicially established. One of the fundamental ways in which at-will termination has been nullified is through the "public policy" exception. This exception to the at-will doctrine derives from the belief that employers should not be able to use their power over employees to violate laws and principles established by other legal bodies for the public good. For example, being fired because you claimed a legislatively created benefit such as workers' compensation, exercised a constitutional right such as voting, or refused to commit an illegal act on behalf of the employer would be considered in most states as grounds for a public policy exception because the action attempts to prevent what federal and state laws have created for the public good (Miceli and Near 1992:240). Whistleblowers who suffer retaliatory actions for disclosing or attempting to stop unlawful or hazardous acts of their employer would be protected in most states under their public policy exception.

The majority of states have adopted a public policy exception to an at-will termination. However, the specific activities and legislative mandates that fall within the domain of public policy are rooted in the case-by-case interpretations of the judicially made common law of each state. A firing in violation of public policy is brought as a wrongful discharge in tort, with the employee entitled to damages for his or her suffering (Miceli and Near 1992:240). Some states proceed with legal action for wrongful discharge as a violation of contract (see Kohn and Kohn 1988). Compared to federal or state statutory remedies, a common law cause of action for wrongful discharge is preferable for most whistleblowers because such claims often provide greater remedies and may involve a longer statute of limitations (BNA 1995).

Federal Statutes

Employees who report organizational or governmental misconduct are not uniformly protected against retaliatory actions under federal law. Instead, federal statutory protection is provided to workers in a largely haphazard fashion. Only specific types of actions by employers and employees within particular industries are covered under federal laws. Each federal whistleblower statute has its own definition of what type of speech rights of employees is protected, its own filing provisions, its own statute of limitations, its own remedies for employees, and its own specified sanctions against violators of the statute (Kohn and Kohn 1988:17). Although each federal statute has unique elements regarding whistleblower protection, the laws are sometimes modeled after each other and share similar provisions in terms of defining employer misconduct, reporting procedures, and remedial action. Depending on the specific federal law involved, whistleblowers' claims are either brought in federal district court or filed with the secretary of labor or another appropriate administrative agency (BNA 1995).

Whistleblower provisions within federal statutes are designed to protect employees from retaliation and to compensate those who have suffered from it. The increased prevalence of statutory protection over the last two decades is due to the growing awareness by Congress and other legal bodies of the importance of whistleblowing for exposing fraud, waste, and abuse in a variety of work environments. In addition to statutory law, the U.S. Constitution also offers whistleblower protection for some public employees (see Kohn and Kohn 1988; Miceli and Near 1992). A summary of the protection given whistleblowers under the U.S. Constitution and some of the particular federal statutes is presented below.[1]

Constitutional Protection. The First and Fourteenth Amendments to the U.S. Constitution prohibit state and local government officials from retaliating against whistleblowers. Protection under the First Amendment covers employees who express dissent either publicly or directly to their supervisors (Kohn and Kohn 1988). A public employee's free speech is protected from retaliation when it bears on a "public concern," not just a "personal interest." Even if the speech or conduct is constitutionally protected,

---

1. The following section draws heavily from the work of BNA (1995, 1996, 1997), Kohn and Kohn (1988:18–33), and Miceli and Near (1992:251–259).

however, employees still have the initial legal burden to demonstrate that their disclosures were a "motivating factor" in the negative employment decision (Kohn and Kohn 1988:19). Some federal workers have more restrictive protection under the First Amendment. For example, the Supreme Court has essentially mandated that federal civil servants must utilize administrative remedies for retaliatory employment practices if they are available and cannot bring an independent tort or civil action against their employer under the First Amendment. Victims of retaliatory discharge may also have no legal protection for otherwise protected free speech because of immunity granted to certain public officials and some governmental bodies. Both compensatory and punitive damages are available in civil litigation by employees wrongfully treated for expressing their constitutional right of free speech.

Environmental Laws.   Whistleblower protection provisions are included for the disclosure of violations of the following federal environmental laws: the Toxic Substances Control Act (15 U.S.C. 2622), the Superfund (42 U.S.C. 9610), the Water Pollution Control Act (33 U.S.C. 1367), the Solid Waste Disposal Act (42 U.S.C. 6971), the Clean Air Act (42 U.S.C. 7622), the Atomic Energy and Energy Reorganization Acts (42 U.S.C. 5851), and the Safe Drinking Water Act (42 U.S.C. 300j-9). Under the employee protection provisions of these acts, no employer may discharge or otherwise discriminate against any employee for commencing, causing, testifying in, assisting in, or participating in proceedings covered by the acts. Environmental whistleblowers must file their complaint with the secretary of the U.S. Department of Labor within thirty days of the adverse job actions. The remedies for wrongful employment actions under these environmental laws are similar to those for whistleblowers covered by other federal statutes: reinstatement, back pay, compensatory damages, and attorneys' fees. There is some debate in court interpretations on whether purely internal whistleblowing to management is statutorily protected under these environmental laws. For example, most circuits of the U.S. Court of Appeals have interpreted the Energy Reorganization Act to be protective of both external whistleblowers and employees in the nuclear industry who disclose alleged violations only to management and other internal sources (Kohn and Kohn 1988:19–20).

Surface Transportation Assistance Act (STAA).   The Surface Transportation Assistance Act protects employee whistleblowers who file a complaint and testify in or cause to be instituted proceedings to enforce rules, regulations, or standards regarding the safety of commercial motor vehicles. Most whistleblowers under this federal statute are truck drivers. These employees have the right to refuse to operate a vehicle, without fear of reprisals, because (1) they have a reasonable belief that operating the vehicle would cause serious injury to the employee or the public and (2) such operation would constitute a violation of any federal rules, regulations, standards or orders applicable to commercial motor vehicle safety or health. Complaints under this act must be filed with the secretary of labor within 180 days of the alleged wrongful employment practice. Upon a preliminary finding of merit, the employee is entitled to immediate temporary reinstatement pending the outcome of a full evidentiary hearing. This provision for temporary rein-statement is extremely important because it lessens the ability of the offending company to use litigation delay to place an extreme financial burden on whistleblowers and reduce their prospects for reemployment. Reinstatement, back pay, compensatory damages, costs, and attorneys' fees are remedies for reprisals against these whistleblowers.

Occupational Safety and Health Act (OSHA). Employees are protected under the Occupational Safety and Health Act from any type of retaliation that derives from disclosures about workplace health and safety. Courts have interpreted this statute to include a right to refuse hazardous work un-der particular circumstances. Employees file their complaint for prohibited conduct with the local OSHA administrative office within thirty days of the time they learned of the reprisals. The allegations are investigated by the secretary of labor. Upon the finding of an OSHA violation, the secretary sues the employer on behalf of the employee for reinstate-ment, back pay, and other remedies. OSHA protection for whistleblowers is different from most other federal laws in this requirement that employees must rely exclusively on an external agent for legal action. Although employees under OSHA do not have a federal statutory right to initiate their own suit for retaliatory discharge, these employees may have a private cause of action for wrongful discharge under their state law. Protection for reporting OSHA violations cov-ers both internal and external sources, including disclosures to the U.S. Department of Labor, unions, management, and newspapers (Kohn and Kohn 1988:23–24). Separate federal statutes also cover the exposure of other health and safety problems. For example, the Asbestos School Hazard Detection Act of 1980 prohibits retaliation against employees who publicly disclose information about a potential asbestos problem in school buildings (BNA 1995).

Federal Mine Health and Safety Act (FMHSA). Administrative remedies for violations of FMHSA are provided to miners, miners' representatives, and applicants for employment in a mine. The purpose of this act is to strengthen the health and safety of miners. Both internal and external whistleblowing complaints are statutorily protected under this act. Workers must file a complaint with the U.S. Department of Labor within sixty days of the alleged retaliatory actions. A review commission is required to process the complaint quickly, and upon a preliminary determination that the complaint was not frivolously brought, the commission must order the immediate reinstatement of the miner pending full adjudication of the complaint. If the secretary of labor rules against the employee, the worker may file a separate complaint with the commission on his or her own behalf. Remedies for successful whistleblowers under FMHSA include reinstatement, back pay, costs, and attorneys' fees (Kohn and Kohn 1988:24–25).

Depository Institution Employee Protection Remedy. The Depository Institution Employee Protection Remedy Act prohibits retaliation against an employee of a depository institution or federal banking agency for reporting to a federal banking agency or to the attorney general a possible violation of law, gross mismanagement, gross waste of funds, abuse of authority, or a substantial and specific danger to public health or safety (BNA 1995).

Department of Defense Authorization Act of 1984 and 1987. The 1984 act prohibits retaliation against civilian employees of the Department of Defense for disclosing violations of laws and regulations, mismanagement, gross waste of funds, abuse of authority, or substantial and specific danger to public health or safety. An administrative investigation is conducted by the secretary of defense, who has authority to correct adverse employment actions (Westman 1991:190). The 1987 act prohibits retaliation against employees of defense contractors who disclose substantial violations of law relating to defense contracts to members of Congress or authorized representatives of the Department of Defense or Justice.

National Labor Relations Act (NLRA). Passed in 1935 as the first legislation that incorporates whistleblower protection, NLRA covers workers in union-related activities who testify or file charges for unfair labor practices. This act has become the model for other employment discrimination laws. It has also been used to eliminate at-will terminations for most unionized employees through the establishment of "just cause" firing provisions in labor contracts. Retaliation complaints have a six-month statute of limitations and must be filed at the nearest regional office of the National Labor Relations Board (NLRB). The NLRB's general counsel has the initial burden of showing that the employee's complaint was a "motivating factor" in his or her adverse employment decision (Miceli and Near 1992:253). Reinstatement and back pay are common remedies for whistleblowers under this law.

Section 301 of the Labor-Management Relations Act and Duty of Fair Representation Claims. Employees under a collective bargaining agreement are protected under the Labor-Management Relations Act from retaliatory discharge if their firing is a violation of the union-management contract. Employees who are wrongfully terminated must exhaust the contractual grievance procedures (such as arbitration) prior to filing a breach of contract claim under Section 301 of the act. When labor unions fail to properly use these grievance procedures, then both the union and employee must be sued under Section 301 according to the "Duty of Fair Representation" (DFR) doctrine. DFR claims provide some protection for whistleblowers who are unpopular with their local unions and consequently have their grievances handled in a largely perfunctory manner (Kohn and Kohn 1988:25–26).

Surface Mining Control and Reclamation Act. Whistleblowers are protected under the Surface Mining Control and Reclamation Act for reporting an alleged environmental violation involving surface mining operations. Complaints must be filed within thirty days to the U.S. Department of Interior. Administrative regulations provide these whistleblowers with temporary relief from retaliatory actions. Remedies for employees protected under this act include reinstatement, back pay, and attorneys' fees (Westman 1991:196).

Job Training and Partnership Act (JTPA). The Job Training and Partnership Act protects employees against retaliation for reporting grant violations or filing a complaint under JTPA. Employees must initially utilize internal grievance procedures for corrective action. After these procedures are exhausted, complaints may be filed directly with the secretary of the Department of Labor (Kohn and Kohn 1988:27).

Employee Retirement Income Security Act (ERISA).   Federal protection under ERISA is given to any person who is retaliated against for participating in an ERISA retirement or benefit plan. Coverage under this act also includes persons who give information or testify concerning ERISA or the Welfare and Pensions Plans Disclosure Act. Complaints of retaliation are filed in federal district court. Court interpretations differ on what constitutes appropriate reporting channels for these complaints. For example, some courts have required ERISA plaintiffs to exhaust administrative remedies prior to filing a suit in federal court (Kohn and Kohn 1988:28). Remedies for retaliatory actions include the recovery of benefits, interest, attorneys' fees, and costs. Administrators who refuse to provide requested information may be held personally liable.

Fair Labor Standards Act (FLSA).   Whistleblower protection covers employees from retaliation for complaining, testifying, or filing charges for violations of the provisions of the Fair Labor Standards Act concerning child labor, minimum wage, and sex discrimination under the Equal Pay Act. Complaints may be filed within two years with the Department of Labor or in a federal or state court. Appropriate remedies for wrongful conduct include employment, reinstatement, promotion, back pay, liquidated damages, and attorneys' fees (Kohn and Kohn 1988:28).

Longshoreman's and Harbor Worker's Compensation Act (LHWCA).   As a maritime worker's compensation law, LHWCA covers workers who are injured on navigable waters of the United States and on piers, wharves, and adjoining areas used for loading, unloading, and building a vessel.

The whistleblower provision shields from retaliation those employees who either claim protection or compensation under the law or testify in a related proceeding (Kohn and Kohn 1988:29). Complaints are filed with the secretary of the Department of Labor after the employer refuses to pay. Employees are entitled to reinstatement and back pay. The violating employer is subject to a civil fine of up to $5,000.

Migrant and Seasonal Agricultural Workers Protection Act. Migrant workers who file a complaint, institute proceedings, testify, or exercise their rights under the Migrant and Seasonal Agricultural Workers Protection statute are given whistleblower protection. Complaints of alleged discrimination must be filed with the secretary of the Department of Labor within 180 days of the employee's first knowledge of the adverse job action. If allegations of a violation are sustained through investigation, the secretary files a suit in federal district court on behalf of the employee. Employees also have legal recourse to file a private cause of action against violators of any provision of this act. Alternative administrative remedies do not have to be exhausted to press this legal action. Reinstatement with back pay, damages, and injunctions are remedies under this act (Kohn and Kohn 1988:29–30; Westman 1991:195).

Safe Containers for International Cargo Act. Employees who disclose a violation of the Safe Containers for International Cargo Act, or who report on the use of unsafe containers in international transport, are protected from retaliation. These complaints must be filed with the secretary of labor within sixty days of the alleged violation. If the charges of retaliation are substantiated by investigation, the secretary files a complaint for "appropriate relief" in federal district court. Remedies for retaliation may include reinstatement and back pay (Miceli and Near 1992:257).

Title VII of the Civil Rights Act of 1991.   Employees who either experience or witness discriminatory practices and file a complaint against them are given some whistleblowing protection under Title VII. Employees' allegations of discriminatory practices under Title VII proceed with the submission of written charges to the Equal Employment Opportunity Commission (EEOC). Upon receipt of a "right to sue" letter from the EEOC, the whistleblower has limited time (usually within ninety days) to file a complaint in federal court for wrongful discharge. Remedies under Title VII may include injunction, reinstatement, back pay, and limited compensatory and punitive damages for intentional discriminatory practices (Kohn and Kohn 1988:30). Similar provisions against retaliation for reporting discriminatory practices are provided under the Age Discrimination in Employment Act, the Fair Labor Standards Act, and, in the case of racial discrimination, Section 1981 of the Civil Rights Act of 1870.

Civil Service Reform Act (CSRA) and the Whistleblower Protection Act (WPA).   Federal whistleblowers are also protected from retaliation under provisions of the Civil Service Reform Act. These protections have been augmented through the passage of the Whistleblower Protection Act of 1989 and its revision in 1994. CSRA prohibits a federal agency from taking an adverse "personnel action" (such as termination, demotion, reassignment, and the failure to hire or promote) against a civil servant in retaliation for both internal and external whistleblowing activities. Employees submit their complaint to the Office of Special Counsel (OSC). The OSC has primary responsibility for investigating the complaint, protecting employees, and defending those who claim they were victimized by prohibited personnel practices. The Whistleblower Protection Act strengthened the OSC as an independent investigative body and increased the protection of whistleblowers by (1) allowing employees to pursue their own cases if the OSC refuses to take the case to the Merit Systems Protection Board and (2) easing the burden of proof for employees to show that their adverse treatment was due to their whistleblowing (Miceli and Near 1992:238). Unfortunately, most commentators view the CSRA and WPA as major failures in protecting the rights of federal workers (see GAP 1997b; Miceli and Near 1992).

The 1986 Amendment to the False Claims Act.   The False Claims Act establishes civil liability against persons or corporations who defraud the government. Given the importance of whistleblowing for exposing fraudulent activities against the government and other entities, the amended act provides some assurances that whistleblowers are protected from retaliation. Complaints of retaliation are filed by the employee in the appropriate federal district court and are covered by a six-year statute of limitations. As long as the allegations of fraud are made in "good faith," whistleblowers are protected even when subsequent investigations reveal no underlying violation of the False Claims Act. Remedies for retaliation under this act are far more substantial than relief provided by other federal statutes. These remedies include reinstatement, compensation for "special damages," double the amount of back pay, and attorneys' fees and costs. As described shortly, the ability of individual whistleblowers under this statute to receive enormous financial awards by filing separate civil claims against their fraudulent employer or subcontractors on behalf of the government is an important special condition of the False Claims Act.

State-Based Approaches for Whistleblower Protection

Nearly all states have some type of whistleblower protection for employees. This protection comes in the form of state statutes and the recognition in most states' common law of a public policy exception to the employment at-will doctrine. The types of employees covered under state statutes vary dramatically across jurisdictions, but these whistleblower laws usually protect only public employees from retaliatory actions. Protection under state laws is further restricted in many instances to the reporting of gross and serious violations of state or federal laws, rules, or regulations (Miceli and Near 1992). In contrast, states that have adopted the judicially derived public policy exception often provide protection to a wider class of employees and have greatly expanded the legal rights of whistleblowers. For example, the public policy exception usually protects all private sector employees from retaliatory actions (not just specific types of workers covered under specific laws). The classification of retaliatory discharge as a tort in most states also gives whistleblowers the legal right to jury trials in state court and the opportunity to seek punitive damages for their injuries (Kohn and Kohn 1988).

The protection of employee whistleblowers under state statutes and the public policy exception has dramatically increased in the last two decades. However, the nature and scope of state-level whistleblowing protection is still evolving. Some states have recently enacted whistleblower protection or are in the process of doing so. Whether or not a state's supreme court has recognized a public policy exception and the definitions of what constitutes "protected activity" are also subject to change over time. Potential whistleblowers are strongly advised to consult lawyers who are well trained in labor law and civil litigation to determine the current status of whistleblower protection for their particular problem.

Based on materials from several sources (see BNA 1997; Kohn and Kohn 1988; Miceli and Near 1992; Westman 1991) and the specific state codes and case law, a state-by-state summary of whistleblower statutes and their respective public policy exceptions to at-will termination is given below.[2] Rather than including the extensive details of each statute and the full text of the common law rulings, only general principles and provisions are presented in this summary. Readers with interest in the specific details of state whistleblowing protection should consult the actual statutes and relevant case law. Table 6.1 summarizes the whistleblower protection and public policy exceptions for each state.

---

2. It is important to note that whistleblowers in all states, like all individuals, are also provided protection under criminal and civil statutes for "witness intimidation," "harassment," and "obstruction of justice." These state laws provide protection for individuals who testify in legal proceedings. The state-based whistleblowing laws examined in this section are restricted to the protection of workers or former workers from retaliatory employment practices. Even if there is no protection for whistleblowers under state statutes or case law, whistleblowers may still be protected under particular provisions of the U.S. Constitution and specific federal statutes.

110

TABLE 6.1   Summary of Public Policy Exceptions to "At-Will" Termination and the Type of Employees Covered by Whistle-blowing Protection Laws in Each State

State	Public Policy Exception?	Type of Employee Protected?	
		Public	Private
Alabama	No	Yes	No
Alaska	Yes	Yes	No
Arizona	Yes	Yes	No
Arkansas	Yes	No	No
California	Yes	Yes	Yes
Colorado	Yes	Yes	No
Connecticut	Yes	Yes	Yes
Delaware	No	Yes	No
Florida	No	Yes	Yes
Georgia	No	Yes	No
Hawaii	Yes	Yes	Yes
Idaho	Yes	No	No
Illinois	Yes	Yes	Yes
Indiana	Yes	Yes	No
Iowa	Yes	Yes	Yes
Kansas	Yes	Yes	No
Kentucky	Yes	Yes	No
Louisiana	Yes	Yes	Yes
Maine	Yes	Yes	Yes
Maryland	Yes	Yes	No
Massachusetts	Yes	Yes	No
Michigan	Yes	Yes	Yes
Minnesota	Yes	Yes	Yes
Mississippi	Yes	No	No
Missouri	Yes	Yes	No

(continues)

TABLE 6.1 *(continued)*

Montana	Yes	Yes	Yes
Nebraska	Yes	No	No
Nevada	Yes	Yes	No
New Hampshire	Yes	Yes	Yes
New Jersey	Yes	Yes	Yes
New Mexico	Yes	No	No
New York	No	Yes	Yes
North Carolina	Yes	Yes	Yes
North Dakota	Yes	Yes	Yes
Ohio	Yes	Yes	Yes
Oklahoma	Yes	Yes	No
Oregon	Yes	Yes	No
Pennsylvania	Yes	Yes	No
Rhode Island	No	Yes	Yes
South Carolina	Yes	Yes	No
South Dakota	Yes	Yes	No
Tennessee	Yes	Yes	Yes
Texas	Yes	Yes	No
Utah	Yes	Yes	No
Vermont	Yes	No	No
Virginia	Yes	No	No
Washington	Yes	Yes	No
West Virginia	Yes	Yes	No
Wisconsin	Yes	Yes	No
Wyoming	Yes	No	No
Total	44	42	19

Source: BNA 1997; Miceli and Near 1992; Westman 1991.

Alabama. State law protects employees and other individuals from being discriminated against as a result of disclosing information, making a charge, or refusing to obey an illegal order. Types of discriminatory treatment of whistleblowers include discharging or otherwise disciplining, threatening, harassing, or blacklisting an employee. Although the Alabama Supreme Court consistently has declined to create a public policy exception to the employment at-will doctrine, an amendment to the workers' compensation statute established a public policy exception when an employee is discharged "solely" for filing a claim for compensation under the statute (BNA 1996).

Alaska. State law protects public employees for reporting violations of local, state, and federal codes. Protected conduct includes the reporting of violations of any law or regulation, danger to public health and safety, gross mismanagement, substantial waste of funds, or clear abuse of authority (Westman 1991). Employees report violations and reprisals in court or to a public body for remedial action. Whistleblowers may bring civil action against the offender, and the court may grant appropriate relief including punitive damages. The Alaska Supreme Court has upheld a public policy exception as a cause of action under contract law, with violations being considered breaches of the implied covenant of good faith and fair dealing (BNA 1997).

Arizona. State or local government employees are statutorily protected from retaliation for reporting violations of any law, mismanagement, gross waste of moneys, or abuse of authority. Sanctions for violators of this statute include suspension from work without pay and termination of employment (Miceli and Near 1992). The Arizona Supreme Court has adopted the public policy exception and has indicated that its protection should be extended to whistleblowers. Under a tort for wrongful discharge, the employee must show that the termination was due to either (1) the refusal to perform some act contrary to public policy or (2) the actual performance of some act that he or she had a right to do as a matter of public policy (Kohn and Kohn 1988:41–42). The Arizona legislature has codified in its Employment Protection Act of 1996 the public policy exception to at-will terminations.

Arkansas. Arkansas has no state statute that protects whistleblowers. However, the state supreme court has recognized the public policy exception and has extended that protection to whistleblowers in some circumstances (Westman 1991:199).

California. Both public and private employees are protected under state statutes for reporting violations of federal or state law or regulations. State government employees are also protected for disclosing economic waste, gross misconduct, incompetency, or inefficiency (Westman 1991). The state statutes impose criminal liability on employers who retaliate against employees who disclose this information, subjecting violators to a fine, imprisonment, or both. California was the first state to adopt the public policy exception to the termination at-will doctrine. The state courts in California have not generally required employees to exhaust administrative remedies prior to the filing of a civil suit for wrongful discharge (Kohn and Kohn 1988:43).

Colorado. Public employees are statutorily protected for reporting actions of state agencies that are not in the public interest. These include the waste of public funds, abuse of authority, and mismanagement (Westman 1991:178). Employees are required to make a "good faith" effort to report misconduct internally to supervisors and appointing authority before external disclosures. A state personnel board investigates and hears the complaint. Employees may sue their employer for reinstatement, back pay, and other relief. The Colorado Supreme Court has formally recognized the public policy exception to at-will termination (BNA 1996).

Connecticut. Both public and private employees are provided statutory protection against retaliation for reporting a wide range of violations. Whistleblowing protection for private employees covers "good faith" reporting of violations of state or federal laws and regulations. Protected disclosures for public employees also include reports of corruption, unethical practices, mismanagement, gross waste of funds, abuse of authority, and danger to public health and safety. Private employees must exhaust all available administrative remedies prior to bringing civil action. Remedies under the state whistleblowing statute include reinstatement with payment of back wages and benefits, court costs, and reasonable attorneys' fees (Westman 1991:183). The Connecticut courts adopt a narrow public policy exception, when the reason for discharge was an "important violation" of public policy (BNA 1996).

Delaware. Public employees under Delaware statutes are protected from being discharged, threatened, or otherwise discriminated against for reporting violations or suspected violations of state or federal law and regulations. Complaints must be filed within ninety days with the state Office of the Auditor of Accounts (Miceli and Near 1992:261). The state courts in Delaware have not specifically recognized a public policy exception to an employer's ability to dismiss an at-will employee (BNA 1996).

Florida. Public employees and those who are employed by independent contractors for state agencies are protected by state statute from retaliation. Protected activities include the reporting of malfeasance and violations of laws, rules, and regulations that present substantial and specific dangers to public health, safety, or welfare (Westman 1991:178). All contractual or administrative remedies must be exhausted before an employee may file civil actions for reinstatement, back pay, and attorneys' fees. Florida courts have not recognized a common law, public policy exception to the at-will doctrine but have created a statutory cause of action where the discharge is in retaliation for filing a workers' compensation claim (BNA 1996).

Georgia. Public employees in Georgia are protected under state statutes from reprisals for reporting fraud, waste, or abuse in state programs and operations. The state courts have not recognized a public policy exception. Under the common law, an at-will employee in Georgia may be terminated with or without cause and regardless of motive.

Hawaii. Both public and private sector employees are protected by state statutes for reporting violations or suspected violations of local, state, or federal laws and rules. Complaints must be filed with a public body within ninety days. Court costs, attorneys' fees, and reinstatement with fringe benefits, seniority rights, and lost wages are remedies for whistleblowers. The Hawaii Supreme Court has recognized the right of an at-will employee to bring a tort action (and subsequently seek punitive damages where appropriate) against an employer for retaliatory discharge. The employee has the burden of proving that the discharge violated a clear mandate of public policy (BNA 1995). When there is conflict between the terms and provisions of statutes and the common law, the provisions that are most beneficial to the employee are utilized.

Idaho.   There is no state statutory protection for whistleblowers in Idaho, but employees may claim damages for wrongful discharge when the firing is motivated to oppose a public policy. Specific examples of public policy exceptions identified by the Idaho Supreme Court include terminations for such reasons as refusing to give false testimony, reporting an injury to file for workers' compensation, refusing to have social relations with a supervisor, and serving on jury duty against an employer's wishes (BNA 1995; Kohn and Kohn 1988:45–46).

Illinois.   Both public and private employees are covered by state statutes for reporting violations of laws or regulations, mismanagement, gross waste of funds, abuse of authority, and substantial and specific dangers to public health and safety. Whistleblowers must report alleged retaliation to the director of the Department of Labor within thirty days of the violation. Separate state statutes enable individuals to file *qui tam* lawsuits against violators of state law. The Illinois Supreme Court has recognized the public policy exception and several different bases for retaliatory claims by whistleblowers (BNA 1996; Westman 1991). Employees may file tort action for retaliatory discharge under the public policy exception or for the intentional infliction of emotional distress.

Indiana. State statutory protection for whistleblowers is provided to public employees, including those employed in state educational institutions, and to persons whose employer is under state contract. Under the State Employees Bill of Rights, no state employee may be dismissed, have benefits withheld, be transferred, or be demoted for reporting in writing the existence of a state, federal, or regulatory violation or the misuse of public resources (Kohn and Kohn 1988:47). Employees initiate this formal complaint through their supervisor or the appointing authority, unless that person is the alleged offender. A public policy exception is recognized by the Indiana Supreme Court only where the employee can demonstrate that the discharge was for exercising a statutory right or complying with a statutory duty (BNA 1995). The plaintiff bears the burden of proving that the discharge was motivated by the expression of this right or duty.

Iowa. Both public and private employees are protected under Iowa statutes for reporting violations of law or rules, mismanagement, gross abuse of funds, abuse of authority, or substantial and specific danger to public health or safety.

The Iowa Supreme Court has recognized a public policy exception to the at-will doctrine. The legal remedy under the exception is a cause of action for retaliatory discharge in violation of public policy, rather than a cause of action for tortious interference with contract (BNA 1997).

Kansas. State statutes protect public employees in Kansas who disclose violations of state or federal laws, rules, and regulations. The Kansas courts have adopted a public policy exception to the termination at-will doctrine, limiting it to interests protected by state law. Punitive damages in tort action for wrongful discharge may be awarded under appropriate circumstances (Kohn and Kohn 1988:48).

Kentucky. Public employees and specific employees of public contractors are provided statutory protection for reporting actual or suspected violations of federal and state law, executive orders, regulations, rules, or ordinances. Specific violations covered under the statute include mismanagement, waste, fraud, and the endangerment of public health or safety. Reporting channels for claims include the state attorney general, the auditor of public accounts, the state's general assembly, or any other appropriate body or authority. Remedies for these whistleblowers include injunctive relief, possible punitive damages, court costs, attorneys' fees, and reinstatement with back pay, fringe benefits, and seniority rights (Miceli and Near 1992:264). Kentucky's supreme court has adopted an exception to the employment at-will doctrine, whenever the discharge is contrary to a fundamental and well-defined public policy (BNA 1997).

Louisiana. Both public and private employees are protected under state statutes for "good faith" reporting of violations of federal, state, or local environmental statute, ordinance, or regulation. Remedies for retaliation against these environmental whistleblowers include treble damages for lost wages and anticipated wages from lost promotions and fringe benefits, physical or emotional distress damages, court costs, and attorneys' fees. Causes of action for violation of the public policy exception exist for Louisiana employees only if they are terminated in violation of rights they have been given by the federal or state constitution or by specific statutes (BNA 1997).

Maine. State statutory law protects both public and private employees who report violations of state and federal laws or rules or a risk to health or safety. Most complaints are filed initially with the employer, and the employer is allowed a reasonable time to take corrective action before the complaint goes forward to a public body. After the exhaustion of administrative remedies, these whistleblowers may take civil action for reinstatement with back pay, benefits, seniority, court costs, and attorneys' fees (Westman 1991:184). The Supreme Judicial Court of Maine has endorsed a "good cause" public policy exception to an at-will employment contract. Termination of an employment contract for whistleblowing is considered a wrongful discharge under this exception because "good cause" relates to no activity other than to the services performed or promised in the contract (Kohn and Kohn 1988:49).

Maryland. State employees are protected for reporting violations of law, rule, or regulations; gross mismanagement; waste of funds; abuse of authority; and substantial and specific dangers to public health or safety. Complaints about retaliation are filed with the secretary of personnel (Miceli and Near 1992:265). The Maryland courts accept tort action for abusive discharge when the motivation for termination contravenes public policy. Both state and federal law can be the basis for the public policy exception. Punitive damages are possible for "abusive discharge" in tort action, whereas statutory remedies for whistleblowers supplement those provided under ordinary state employment grievance procedures (Kohn and Kohn 1988:49).

Massachusetts. Public employees are protected from retaliatory actions for disclosures (or threats of such disclosures) to a supervisor or public body of an activity, policy, or practice that the employee reasonably believes is a violation of law or rule or poses a risk to public health, safety, or the environment. Whistleblowers must institute a civil action within two years of the violation. Remedies include (1) restraining orders, (2) reinstatement of the same position, fringe benefits, and seniority rights, and (3) compensation for three times the lost wages, benefits, and interest. A public policy exception to at-will termination has been recognized by the state courts under contract law.

Michigan. Both public and private employees are protected by state statute for reporting violations of state and federal laws, regulations, or rules. Whistleblowers may bring civil action within ninety days for reinstatement, back pay, court costs, attorneys' fees, and civil fine (Westman 1991:184). Michigan courts have adopted a limited public policy exception to termination at-will. This exception applies only when employees are discharged in violation of a "clearly articulated, well accepted public policy," including the expression of a right conferred by statute and the refusal to violate a law in the course of employment. Protected disclosures under the Michigan Whistleblowers' Protection Act of 1981 are also included as part of this public policy exception (Kohn and Kohn 1988:50). The court considers the state's whistleblower law an exclusive remedy for retaliation due to whistleblowing, precluding any claim under the common law (BNA 1995).

Minnesota. Both public and private employees are statutorily protected for reporting violations of any federal and state law or rule and for refusing to participate in these violations. Complaints are filed with a governmental body or a law enforcement official. Upon receipt of a written request from the employee, the employer has five days to notify the whistleblower of the reasons for the involuntary termination (Miceli and Near 1992:265). Tort action for wrongful discharge has been upheld in the Minnesota courts under the public policy exception to the employment at-will doctrine. Remedies for wrongful discharge include damages, court costs, attorneys' fees, and appropriate equitable relief.

Mississippi. Mississippi has no clear and unambiguous statutory protection for whistleblowers. Some statutes that govern public employees require "good cause" for discharging workers, but other statutes in the Mississippi code permit termination of public employees with no cause (see Kohn and Kohn 1988:51). The Mississippi Supreme Court has adopted a narrow public policy exception to at-will termination, when the employee is discharged for refusing to participate in an illegal act (BNA 1997).

Missouri. Public employees are protected under state statute for disclosing violations of any law, rule, and regulation; mismanagement; gross waste of funds; abuse of authority; or a substantial and specific danger to public health or safety. Whistleblowers appeal adverse employment practices to the state personnel advisory board or appropriate agency or review board (Miceli and Near 1992:266). The Missouri courts have upheld a public policy exception against at-will firing, protecting employees from discharge for refusing to violate a statute, reporting violations of the law by employers or co-workers, or asserting a legal right (BNA 1996).

Montana. State statutory protection is extended to both public and private employees who report violations of public policy in the areas of health, safety, and welfare. Whistleblowers must exhaust internal procedures before initiating other action. Punitive damages are possible in lawsuits when fraud or malice by the employer is present in the wrongful discharge (Miceli and Near 1992:267). A public policy cause of action has been adopted by the Montana Supreme Court. Examples of conduct in clear violation of public policy listed by the court include terminating employees for refusing to perjure themselves, asserting their right to workers' compensation benefits, and refusing sexual relations (Kohn and Kohn 1988:51–52).

Nebraska. Nebraska has no state statute for protecting whistleblowers. The Nebraska Supreme Court recognizes a limited public policy exception for the at-will doctrine, when it violates a constitutional or statutory prohibition (BNA 1997).

Nevada. State employees are protected under Nevada statutes from reprisals for reporting improper governmental action. This misconduct includes violations of any state law and regulation, an abuse of authority of a substantial and specific danger to the public health and safety, or a gross waste of public money. Nevada courts have supported a public policy exception to termination at-will. Conduct is against public policy when certain behaviors are explicitly forbidden under state statutes. Punitive damages are possible under a tort action for retaliatory discharge if the plaintiff can demonstrate malicious, oppressive, or fraudulent conduct on the part of the defendant (Kohn and Kohn 1988:52).

New Hampshire. Both public and private employees are protected under state statutes for reporting violations of local, state, and federal laws and rules and for refusal to participate in these violations. Unless they have reasonable fear of physical harm, whistleblowers must first report the retaliation to their superiors and allow a reasonable opportunity for corrective action. A hearing with the commissioner of labor is held after all internal procedures and remedies are exhausted. Employees who are wrongfully terminated are entitled to injunctive relief, reinstatement with benefits and seniority, court costs, and attorneys' fees (Miceli and Near

1992:267). The New Hampshire Supreme Court has adopted a public policy exception to the at-will doctrine. For successful tort action for wrongful discharge, the whistleblower must show that the employer was motivated by bad faith, malice, or retaliation and must demonstrate that the discharge violated public policy (Kohn and Kohn 1988:53).

New Jersey. The state statute protects both public and private employees who disclose allegations of wrongdoing to a public body. Employees are generally required to first report the retaliatory actions to their supervisors and allow them a reasonable opportunity to take corrective action. An employee who uses this whistleblower statute waives the right to pursue other remedies. Wrongfully treated whistleblowers are eligible for injunctive relief, court costs, attorneys' fees, possible punitive damages, and reinstatement with benefits, seniority, and full back pay (Westman 1991:185). New Jersey courts recognize a public policy exception as grounds for wrongful discharge in both contract and tort actions. The source of public policy includes legislation (administrative rules, regulations, or decisions) and judicial opinions (BNA 1996; Kohn and Kohn 1988:53).

New Mexico. New Mexico has no state statutory protection of whistleblowers. The state courts, however, have adopted a public policy exception to the at-will doctrine. Employees who are involved in tort action for retaliatory or abusive discharge must demonstrate that they were terminated because they performed an act that public policy had authorized or that they refused to do something required of them that public policy would condemn (BNA 1997).

New York. Both public and private employees are covered by several state statutes for reporting violations of laws, rules, or regulations that create a substantial and specific danger to public health and safety. Public employees are also protected for reporting improper governmental activity. Employees must initiate complaints with their supervisor or appointing authority and give them reasonable time to take appropriate action (Westman 1991:185–186). Injunction, court costs, attorneys' fees, possible punitive damages, and reinstatement with fringe benefits, seniority rights, and back pay are remedies for these whistleblowers. New York does not recognize a tort cause of action for abusive or wrongful discharge in violation of public policy (BNA 1995).

North Carolina. State statutes provide whistleblower protection for public and private employees who report violations of state and federal laws, rules, and regulations; fraud; misappropriation of state funds; and a danger to public health and safety. Complaints are filed with supervisors, department heads, and other appropriate authorities. Whistleblowers are eligible for damages, injunction, or other remedies against the offending person or agency, including court costs, attorneys' fees, and reinstatement with back pay, fringe benefits, and seniority rights. Employees are entitled to treble damages, costs, and attorneys' fees if the court finds that the employer willfully violated the statute (Miceli and Near 1992:268). Although an employer can terminate an at-will employee for no reason or for an arbitrary or irrational reason, it cannot do so for an unlawful reason or for a purpose that contravenes public policy (BNA 1996).

North Dakota. Both public and private sector employees are statutorily protected from reprisals for reporting violations of law, regulations, and rules. As in some other states (for instance, Florida, New York, and North Carolina), whistleblowing protection in this state also covers opposing or refusing to participate in an activity believed to be a violation of law (GAP 1997b). North Dakota courts have recognized a limited public policy exception to at-will termination, when an employee files a workers' compensation claim or responds to a subpoena (BNA 1995).

Ohio. Both public and private employees are protected under state codes for reporting violations of state and federal statutes, ordinances, or regulations that the employer has authority to correct and that the employee believes are criminal offenses likely to cause imminent risk of physical harm or a hazard to public health and safety. The complaint begins with an oral report to a supervisor or other responsible officer, followed by a detailed written report. Remedies for whistleblowers include court costs, attorneys' fees, injunctive relief, and reinstatement with back wage, fringe benefits, and seniority (Miceli and Near 1992:269; Westman 1991:186). The Ohio Supreme Court has recognized a public policy exception to at-will terminations. Such an exception for a "clear public policy" includes federal and state constitutions, legislation, administrative rules and regulations, and common law (BNA 1997).

Oklahoma. Public employees are protected by state statutes from retaliation for disclosing any information to a

member of the legislature, legislative committee, administrative hearing, or court of law (Westman 1991:180). The
Oklahoma Supreme Court has recognized a judicially created public policy exception to the at-will employment document. The court has held that at-will employees have a
cause of action in tort for wrongful discharge when they are
discharged for refusing to violate an established and well-
defined public policy (BNA 1997).

Oregon. State employees and those employed by public
corporations are protected under state statutes for reporting a variety of misconduct. Complaints are filed through
reports to an independent agency, the supervisor, or an
agency designee. Remedies include injunctive relief and
damages up to $250 (Miceli and Near 1992:269). Oregon
courts recognize a public policy exception to at-will termination. Appropriate public policy actions include being discharged for fulfilling a societal obligation and for pursuing
private statutory rights. When adequate statutory remedies
exist, an additional common law remedy of wrongful discharge may not be upheld (Kohn and Kohn 1988:55–56).

Pennsylvania. State or local governmental employees are
protected under state statute for reporting substantial violations of federal, state, and local statutes, regulations, or a
code of conduct or ethics designed to protect public interests. Violations are reported to a superior, an agent of the
employer, or an appropriate authority. Relief for wrongfully treated employees who are successful in civil action
includes actual damages, court costs, attorneys' fees, in-

junctive relief, and reinstatement with back wages and seniority. The Pennsylvania Supreme Court has upheld a
public policy exception in the wrongful discharge claim of
an at-will employee. Public policy can be derived from the
state constitution, federal law, or state law (Kohn and Kohn
1988:56). The burden of proof is on the employee to show
that some public policy was threatened and that the termination of employment was due to the refusal to perform an
illegal act or for engaging in an act protected by public policy. However, a discharge is considered lawful if the employer can show a separate, plausible, and legitimate reason for firing the employee (Kohn and Kohn 1988:56).

Rhode Island.   State statutory protection for whistleblowing is provided to public employees and to some groups of
private employees whose employer receives public funding and who report violations of laws regarding toxic
waste. These workers are protected for reporting violations
of state, federal, and local laws, rules, and regulations to a
public body. Injunctive relief, actual damages, litigation
costs, and reinstatement with back wages, fringe benefits,
and seniority rights are possible remedies for adverse employment action against whistleblowers in this state. Public
policy exceptions to termination at-will have not been upheld by the Rhode Island courts. There is no cause of action
for wrongful discharge in Rhode Island, and no exception
to the employment at-will doctrine exists for retaliation
against whistleblowers (BNA 1995).

South Carolina.   Public employees are statutorily protected
for reporting violations of any state and federal law or reg-

ulation, governmental criminality, corruption, waste, fraud, gross negligence, or mismanagement. Remedies for wrongful discharge and retaliation include damages, court costs, attorneys' fees, a public "savings" fee up to $2,000, and reinstatement with back pay, fringe benefits, and seniority (Miceli and Near 1992:271). A public policy exception to atwill termination has been upheld in the South Carolina Supreme Court. The plaintiff must demonstrate that the retaliatory discharge opposes a clear mandate of public policy (Kohn and Kohn 1988:57).

South Dakota. Public employees are protected from discharge or the threat of reprisals for filing a complaint, discrimination, or attempting to institute any proceeding. The South Dakota courts have adopted a public policy exception, limited to cases in which an employee is discharged for refusing to commit a criminal or unlawful act (BNA 1996).

Tennessee. Both public and private employees are protected under state statutes from discharge or termination for refusing to participate in, or for refusing to remain silent about, illegal activities. Illegal activities include violations of criminal or civil codes and any regulation intended to protect public health, safety, and welfare. The state supreme court has upheld a tort action for wrongful discharge based on public policy. The court has also determined that punitive damages are possible under a retaliatory discharge tort (Kohn and Kohn 1988: 57).

Texas. Public employees are protected by state statute from suspension, termination, or other forms of discrimination because they have, in good faith, reported violations of the law to an appropriate law enforcement authority. Whistleblowers must initiate any local grievance procedures before they file a civil suit. Remedies for retaliatory discharge include injunctive relief, actual and punitive damages, court costs, attorneys' fees, payment of lost wages, and reinstatement of fringe benefits and seniority rights. The Texas courts have established a public policy exception to the at-will doctrine. The Texas Supreme Court has ruled that employment terminations that violate public policy as expressed in state and federal laws serve as a basis for causes of action for wrongful discharge. However, the employee must demonstrate, by a preponderance of evidence, that the discharge was for no reason other than refusal to perform an illegal act (BNA 1996).

Utah. Public employees are given state statutory protection for disclosing violations of laws, rules, and regulations or waste of public funds, property, or manpower. Most complaints are initiated with a written notice to the employer or by following the employer's administratively established procedures. Employees wrongfully treated are eligible for damages, court costs, attorneys' fees, injunctive relief, and reinstatement with back pay, benefits, and seniority rights (Miceli and Near 1992:271). The Utah Supreme Court has adopted a narrow public policy exception. Actions for wrongful discharge must involve substantial and important public policies, generally including prior legislative pronouncements or judicial decisions in which there is virtually no question as to their importance for the promotion of the public good (BNA 1996).

Vermont. Vermont has no statutory protection of employee whistleblowers. The Vermont courts, however, have developed a broad public policy exception to the termination at-will doctrine that goes beyond statutory directives in defining protected conduct (see BNA 1996; Kohn and Kohn 1988:58).

Virginia. Virginia has no statutory protection of whistleblowers. The state supreme court has recognized a public policy exception to the at-will rule by allowing tort action for improper discharge (Kohn and Kohn 1988). The public policy exception has been applied to cases involving whistleblowers (Westman 1991).

Washington. Public employees are protected by state statute for reporting violations of state law or rules, abuse of authority, gross waste of public funds, or substantial and specific danger to public health and safety. Complaints of retaliatory action are reported to the Office of the State Auditor. The Washington courts have also recognized tort action for wrongful discharge when the dismissal violated a clear mandate of public policy that is either judicially or legislatively recognized. The employee has the initial burden to plead and prove that the conduct violates this clear mandate (BNA 1996).

West Virginia. Public employees are statutorily protected for reporting waste and wrongdoing of more than a technical or minimal nature that violates federal, state, or local statutes, regulations, or ordinances. Codes of conduct and ethics designed to protect the public or employer's interest are also included. Complaints of misconduct are reported to the employer or another appropriate authority. Remedies for whistleblowers include injunctive relief, actual damages, court costs, attorneys' fees, and reinstatement with back wages, benefits, and seniority. Violators may face a civil fine of $500 and suspension for up to six months (Miceli and Near 1992:272). The West Virginia courts have upheld a tort action for retaliatory discharge when the employer's motivation for discharge runs contrary to a "substantial" public policy principle. Sources of public policy include precepts in the constitution, legislative enactments, and judicial opinions (BNA 1995).

Wisconsin.   Public employees are protected by state statute for reporting violations of state or federal law, rules, or regulations; mismanagement; abuse of authority; substantial waste of public funds; and danger to public health and safety. Complaints are initiated through a written notice to the supervisor, an appropriate governmental unit, or a law enforcement agency. The Wisconsin Supreme Court has adopted a narrow public policy exception to employment at-will doctrine, holding that an employee has a cause of action for wrongful discharge when the discharge is "contrary to a fundamental and well-defined public policy as evidenced by existing law" (BNA 1996).

Wyoming.   Wyoming has no state statutory protection for employees who are whistleblowers. However, Wyoming courts have adopted a limited public policy exception to the termination at-will doctrine. The public policy claim has been recognized for employees who file workers' compensation claims (Westman 1991:211).

The False Claims Act
and *Qui Tam* Lawsuits

Most federal and state legislation on whistleblowing focuses on protection against employer retaliation. This focus derives from a reasonable assumption: If employees are to be encouraged as public saviors and report fraud, waste, and abuse, often at great personal costs, then the government should at least provide some legal protection against disgruntled and vindictive employers. Over the last decade, however, there has been a growing recognition that legal protection against retaliatory actions provides neither an adequate remedial action to encourage whistleblowing nor a sufficient threat to organizations and individuals to deter them from various types of misconduct.

The potential for whistleblower legislation to encourage the reporting of organizational misconduct and to serve as a major deterrent for further violations has been revolutionized by revisions to the False Claims Act. Signed into law originally by President Lincoln in 1863 to stop war profiteers from selling substandard supplies to the Union Army at grossly inflated prices, this federal statute established civil liability against individuals or corporations who defraud the government. Subsequent revisions in 1986 strengthen the rewards for citizens to expose and fight fraudulent organizational practices.

Compared to other statutes that protect only a limited class of workers or offer modest financial remedies for wrongful conduct, the False Claims Act has strong provisions against retaliatory discharge and lucrative financial incentives for exposing fraudulent activity. Under particular conditions, whistleblowers may receive multi-million-dollar financial rewards for their disclosures under federal statute. A summary of some of the largest awards was presented in Chapter 5.

A wide range of fraudulent practices against the government is covered under the False Claims Act. These include (1) knowingly presenting, or causing to be presented, a false or fraudulent claim for payment to the federal government; (2) knowingly using, or causing to be used, a false record or statement to get a claim paid by the federal government; (3) conspiring with others to get a false or fraudulent claim paid by the federal government; and (4) knowingly using, or causing to be used, a false record or statement to conceal, avoid, or decrease an obligation to pay money or transmit property to the federal government (TAF 1996:10). Whistleblowers on these false claims for federal funds are protected against retaliation for investigating, initiating, testifying, or assisting in actions filed under the statute.

The most influential provision of the False Claims Act is the opportunity for public citizens with evidence of fraud against federal programs or contracts to sue the violator on behalf of the U.S. government. In these *qui tam* lawsuits,[3] the government has the right to intervene and join the action. However, if the government declines to join the lawsuit, the whistleblower can still proceed with the civil action as a private plaintiff. A chronology of events in a typical *qui tam* case is outlined in Figure 6.1.

The amount of the award given to the whistleblower under *qui tam* lawsuits depends on several factors. For exam-

---

3. *Qui tam* is a Latin phrase that translates as "he who brings an action for the king as well as for himself" (Miceli and Near 1992).

FIGURE 6.1   The Chronology of a Typical *Qui Tam* Case

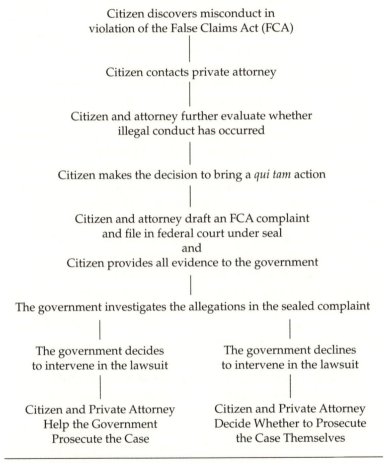

Citizen discovers misconduct in
violation of the False Claims Act (FCA)

Citizen contacts private attorney

Citizen and attorney further evaluate whether
illegal conduct has occurred

Citizen makes the decision to bring a *qui tam* action

Citizen and attorney draft an FCA complaint
and file in federal court under seal
and
Citizen provides all evidence to the government

The government investigates the allegations in the sealed complaint

The government decides
to intervene in the lawsuit

The government declines
to intervene in the lawsuit

Citizen and Private Attorney
Help the Government
Prosecute the Case

Citizen and Private Attorney
Decide Whether to Prosecute
the Case Themselves

Source: TAF (1997). Reprinted by permission of Taxpayers Against
Fraud.

ple, if the government joins the civil suit, and the fraud is proven, the citizen plaintiff can receive between 15 and 25 percent of the total recovery. The successful whistleblower (called the "relator" in these lawsuits) is eligible for between 25 and 30 percent of the proceeds from a judgment or settlement when the government fails to join the lawsuit. Violators of the False Claims Act are liable for three times the dollar amount that the government is defrauded and civil penalties of $5,000 to $10,000 for each false claim. Relators are able to use this treble of damages as the basis for their recovery award. Attorneys' fees for the whistleblower are also recovered in successful *qui tam* suits. The large civil penalties and provisions for treble damages may serve as a powerful deterrent for those individuals and organizations that are contemplating fraud against government programs and contracts. The strong financial incentives for whistleblowers also increase the likelihood of public disclosure of misconduct and the greater scrutiny of organizational practices.

There are several restrictions on the availability and nature of *qui tam* suits and recoveries for whistleblowers. For example, the court can reduce the private plaintiff's share of the recovery if it is determined that the plaintiff was involved in the wrongdoing. If someone else has previously filed a lawsuit or helps to publicize similar allegations, individuals may lose their right to bring a *qui tam* suit. During the time the complaint is under review by the U.S. Justice Department, the whistleblower is under a gag order. The court may dismiss the case if the whistleblower "breaks the seal" by talking to the press (GAP 1997b). The high costs of litigation in false claims suits and the long delay in resolving these cases are other restrictions on this type of whistleblower protection.

The number of cases filed under the False Claims Act and the amount of recoveries have increased dramatically over the last decade. There were 274 cases filed in 1995, involving recoveries of more than $240 million. Recoveries from the False Claims Act exceeded $1 billion for the period from 1987 to 1995 (Phillips and Cohen 1996). Defense contract fraud and health care fraud are the most common types of violations under the False Claims Act.

Aside from the federal False Claims Act, several states (e.g., California, Florida, Illinois) have statutes that enable whistleblowers to recover monetary awards through civil action against defendants who commit frauds on state and local governments. The nature and structure of these state statutory provisions are similar to the federal legislation.

Strengths and Weaknesses of Legal Remedies for Whistleblowers

The legal protection for whistleblowers through statutes and judicial interpretations of common law principles has grown dramatically over the last two decades. Individually and collectively, however, these legal remedies have both strengths and weaknesses. Some of the positive and negative aspects of whistleblower litigation are fundamentally inherent to any legal solution to social problems, whereas other strengths and weaknesses stem from the particular nature and context of whistleblowing.

The most obvious strength of legal approaches to whistleblowing is that they provide some basic protection to workers who disclose organizational abuses. Prior to this protective legislation and the judicially derived exceptions to the employment at-will doctrine, most employees lived in the constant threat of immediate termination by arbitrary and ruthless employers. Speaking out against organizational abuses when employers have unlimited power is professional suicide and a guaranteed career move to the unemployment line. However, even the most nebulous and impotent whistleblowing laws are better than nothing, because they (1) ultimately challenge employers or organizations to think twice about continuing illegal or unethical practices, and (2) place some restrictions on employers' ability to apply the "squawk and walk" rule.

The weaknesses of legal remedies for whistleblowing are wide and varied but fall into two general categories. There are problems inherent with legal solutions in general and problems with specific processes and provisions in whistleblower laws.

Legal solutions to social problems are often fundamentally flawed on several grounds. First, legal remedies are expensive in terms of their economic costs. Attorneys' fees, expert witness expenses, and general court costs may be recovered in many civil cases, but these costs may place an extreme financial burden through the long and tumultuous process of legal relief. For *qui tam* lawsuits involving major fraud, however, attorneys are often retained on a contingency basis, reducing some of the financial burden to the plaintiff. Second, legal solutions are rarely quick fixes and are often extremely taxing in both time and energy. Civil court dockets in many states are filled for years in advance, and the trials and tribulations that often characterize legal action may wear heavily on the physical and psychological well-being of individual plaintiffs. Corporate and organizational defendants are able to use their greater power and resource base to prolong litigation and subsequently add to the emotional and economic burden to the individual plaintiff. Third, legal action is complex and filled with uncertainty. Individuals may expend a considerable amount of money and emotional energy before they find out that their complaint has no legal standing or that the employer's actions were legally justified. The outcome of the most straightforward and obvious complaint is even unpredictable in the world of legal liability.

As for specific problems with the particular components and provisions of whistleblower legislation and case law, the type and nature of these limitations are also wide and varied. The most common criticism of whistleblower statutes and legal remedies include the following (see Miceli and Near 1992; Kohn and Kohn 1988):

- There is no comprehensive and uniform provision for whistleblower protection that applies to all workers, resulting in whistleblower protection being available to only particular types of workers, in particular industries, and in particular jurisdictions.
- There is a preoccupation with a specific type of retaliation (i.e., termination of employment) when other types of adverse employment practices (e.g., collateral involuntary reassignment, less worker autonomy, ostracism, loss of co-worker support) are more

common responses to whistleblowing but are not protected.

- Whistleblowing protection provisions are not adequately enforced by designated regulatory bodies (e.g., the Office of Special Counsel under the Civil Service Reform Act).

- Whistleblowers do not enjoy a generalized federal protection in reporting of misconduct, and whistleblowing is often viewed as an aberrant act valued only if it pertains to certain activities (Miceli and Near 1995:234).

- The short statute of limitations (thirty to ninety days in many cases) severely restricts whistleblowers' access to legal remedies.

- Many state and federal statutes require that all administrative remedies be exhausted before court action or that the statutory provisions (which typically offer less damages) must be sought instead of tort remedies for wrongful discharge.

- Overly restrictive provisions in federal and state statutes nullify the legal standing of a complaint when the whistleblower does not follow proper reporting channels for internal and external disclosures.

- There are too strong burden of proof requirements placed on individual plaintiffs to demonstrate that the wrongful discharge was solely motivated to circumvent public policy.

- The typical legal remedies for whistleblowers, such as reinstatement, back pay, and restoration of benefits, do not present a sufficient incentive to encourage employees to become whistleblowers.

- Employers have successfully limited the likelihood and magnitude of damages in whistleblowing lawsuits for wrongful discharge by arguing that the lawsuit action is preempted by a federal or state statute that offers protection to whistleblowers.

From the whistleblower's perspective, the best protective legislation covers all employees and has a long (two- to five-year) statute of limitations, no requirement for reporting misconduct in a particular way or for first exhausting all administrative remedies, no burden of proof requirement on the whistleblower, stiff criminal penalties and civil fines for violators, and both compensatory and punitive damages against the employer for wrongful conduct. Unfortunately, these combined features are not currently found in any state or federal model of whistleblowing protection.

Effectiveness of
Legal Remedies for Whistleblowing

The effectiveness of any reform effort, in large part, depends upon one's perspective. From the whistleblower's perspective, the question of effectiveness centers on whether the wrongful conduct was terminated and whether there was appropriate compensation and some vindication for the employee's disclosures. From the perspective of wider society, the bottom line on effectiveness is whether whistleblower laws encourage people to report misconduct and, if so, whether this greater public scrutiny ultimately decreases organizational deviance.

Legal Outcomes in Favor of Whistleblower Plaintiffs

It is difficult, if not impossible, to determine the frequency of successful litigation by whistleblowers. This is the case because (1) the majority of complaints are dismissed prior to formal legal action, (2) most formal complaints are settled out of court, with the nature of the settlement being sealed from public scrutiny, and (3) most complaints are grievable through a variety of formal adjudicative bodies (e.g., personnel offices, directory boards, criminal and/or civil courts), creating a major problem with classifying a case as a "success" when a complaint may be upheld in one forum but not in another. Even if comprehensive data were available, there are unresolvable questions about whether "winning" after years of multiple appeals, or when punitive damages are not awarded, or when a person's life has been totally destroyed by the legal process, is actually "winning." Abstract judgments about receiving "appropriate" compensation and vindication for their actions are also difficult to categorize in these terms.

Although defining and measuring success are highly subjective and problematic processes, there is indirect, and limited direct, evidence that full statutory protection is actually given to only a minority of whistleblowers. The most compelling *indirect* evidence to support this claim is the observation that organizations, in general, are more successful as both plaintiffs and defendants than are individuals (Galanter 1974). Studies of discrimination at colleges and universities, for example, report that faculty members who sue their institutions over sex discrimination have only a one-in-five chance of winning their case (*Chronicle of Higher*

Education 1989). Favorable verdicts for whistleblowers, as individual plaintiffs against corporate defendants, are also probably the major exception rather than the rule. The limited success of whistleblowers and other individuals involved in legal disputes with organizations is explained by the dramatic differences in power, financial and auxiliary resources, and legal experiences between most individuals and organizations.

The *direct* evidence for the assertion that few whistleblowers receive legal protection in actual practice comes from evaluations of particular statutes and in particular types of employment situations. Consider the following observations:

- Under the Civil Service Reform Act, the protection against reprisals for federal employees is left entirely to the OSC. Unfortunately, even with major revamping of whistleblower protection under this act, the OSC continues to turn down about 99 percent of its whistleblower cases without attempting corrective action. For example, the OSC filed formal complaints and sought relief for violations of the Whistleblower Protection Act for only 3 employees out of 603 whistleblowing cases it was working on in 1995. A total of 12 complaints out of 662 cases were filed in 1994, and OSC has continued its seventeen-year pattern of not litigating a single reprisal case before the Merit Board to restore a whistleblower's job (GAP 1997b:131).

- Although a growing number of *qui tam* lawsuits have been filed over the last decade (increasing from thirty-three in 1987 to 360 in 1996), these complaints scratch only the surface of a huge iceberg of fraudulent practices against the government in contemporary U.S. society and subsequently provide protection and remedies for only a small number of whistleblowers.

- Successful legal action for reprisals due to reporting OSHA violations is uncommon. In 1990, a total of 3,526 complaints was made to OSHA; evidence of discrimination was found by the Department of Labor in 539 of these cases, but only 21 of them were filed in court (GAP 1997b:138).

- Survey results from more than thirteen federal workers in 1992 indicate that fear of reprisals is a major reason why people who observe organizational misconduct do not report it. A majority of federal workers in that survey who reported an opinion also did not believe that the Civil Service Reform Act would improve their situation if they blew the whistle and were retaliated against (see MSPB 1993). Combined, these results indicate little public confidence in the protective value of this type of whistleblowing legislation.

- Most employees prefer to remain anonymous in their reporting of organizational misconduct. Personal interviews with potential whistleblowers and the widespread use of anonymous hot lines for reporting violations support this observation. One reasonable explanation for the preference for anonymity is the fear of reprisals that may occur because of inadequate legal protection of whistleblowers who are identified by their employer.

Legal Protection and
Controlling Organizational Misconduct

As mentioned in previous chapters, organizational and occupational misconduct is widespread in contemporary society. The traditional approach to crime control for these offenses involves increasing the certainty and severity of punishment for violators. Auditing reports and on-site inspections are common strategies for uncovering occupational deviance, whereas increased jail time and fines proportional to profit are often touted as fundamental ways of increasing the severity of punishment for these offenders.

Over the last two decades, there has been a growing recognition by scholars and legislators of the fundamental importance of whistleblowing in exposing and controlling fraud, waste, and abuse. The growth in statutory protection of whistleblowing in a variety of jurisdictions and employment contexts has been motivated in large part by this observation. However, an important question remains about the effectiveness of whistleblowing laws as a social control mechanism: Does the potential fear of exposure of wrongdoing by whistleblowers diminish the prevalence of organizational misconduct?

Empirical data are not available to establish a definitive causal link between the growth of whistleblowing and the reduction in organizational misconduct. However, information about the motivations and opportunities for organizational misconduct can be used to evaluate the potential success of particular whistleblowing statutes, and whistleblowing in general, in controlling illegal and unethical behavior.

Threat of legal action serves as a deterrent for deviant behavior when punishment is certain and severe. Since whistleblowing, by definition, involves the disclosure of misconduct to some other individual or agency, it obviously increases the public exposure of the wrongful conduct and the subsequent risks of being apprehended for doing it. Likewise, more severe punishment for misconduct has a greater deterrent value than mild punishment because it increases the costs of offending.

From a deterrence perspective, the poor performance of statutory protections against whistleblower retaliation in reducing this misconduct can be attributed to either the low certainty or severity of punishment, or both. Specifically, employers may feel a certain level of invisibility against exposure of misconduct because they wield enormous power to silence dissent from workers. Even if they feel that an employee may expose their misconduct, employers may not be deterred from engaging in prohibited practices because they perceive that the typical punishment for violations (such as reinstatement and back wages) is both minimal and remote.

Of the various whistleblowing statutes, the provisions under the False Claims Act have the clearest potential for controlling organizational misconduct. Two aspects of this law make it an especially powerful deterrent: (1) There is a major financial incentive (up to 30 percent of the total recovery) for employees to expose this type of misconduct, and (2) the financial penalties for False Claim violations are severe (treble the damages and up to a $10,000 fine for each violation). Other whistleblowing statutes, however, are less effective because they lack severe punishment for violators and have minimal incentives to increase the public exposure of fraud, waste, and abuse.

If organizational misconduct is motivated by a rational weighing of the relative costs and benefits of alternative courses of action, the False Claims Act has enormous potential to curtail various types of fraud. When all employees have a major financial interest in reporting violations and the punishment for getting caught is extreme, the costs for doing this type of illegal business are too high. As a result of the continued enforcement of these whistleblower laws, some organizations may desist entirely in their wrongful behavior. However, some organizations may develop alternative ways of generating illegal profits, and other organizations and individuals within them will continue to engage in government fraud even when the risks are high. Nonetheless, the threat of severe and certain punishment under the False Claims Act provides a major hammer that should limit the prevalence of this type of fraud.

Summary

Whistleblowing laws and protection against retaliation vary across different types of employees, industries, and jurisdictions. There are statutory protections for whistleblowers in state and federal codes and protections in the common law under the public policy exceptions to the termination at-will doctrine. Unfortunately, most legal protection for whistleblowers is illusory; few whistleblowers are protected from retaliatory actions because of numerous loopholes and special conditions of these laws and the major disadvantage that individual plaintiffs have against corporate defendants. Among the various types of whistle-blowing protection, the False Claims Act is an especially powerful piece of legislation because it provides a major economic incentive for reporting fraud against the government and has severe civil penalties for offenders.

7

Case Histories of
Six Whistleblowers

As illustrated in previous chapters, survey data provide a general profile of the extent, correlates, and consequences of whistleblowing. Unfortunately, this statistical profile does not capture the full experience of being a whistleblower. Detailed case histories of six whistleblowers are presented in this chapter to illustrate the trials and tribulations of disclosing organizational misconduct.

Mike Quint and
the Los Angeles Subway Tunnels

Efforts to improve the transportation system of Los Angeles have resulted in the largest public works project in the country. Construction of the Metro Rail mass-transit system began in the late 1980s with nearly $200 billion earmarked for the project. The centerpiece of the 59-mile Metro Rail system is the Red Line, a nearly 20-mile subway that will eventually run from Union Station in downtown Los Angeles to North Hollywood (Davis 1994). As of June 1998, approximately 6 miles of the Red Line had been completed.

The first subway tunnels on the Red Line were opened in January 1993.

Building tunnels is always an expensive and dangerous activity, but these problems are compounded in southern California for several obvious reasons. For one thing, as made readily apparent in the Northridge earthquake in January 1994, Los Angeles is prime earthquake territory. Small tremors are an almost daily experience, and the threat of the "big one" is a lingering concern for residents. Another problem is that leaks from corrosive water and natural gases (such as methane and hydrogen sulfide) pose a serious threat to the structural integrity of the tunnel and the safety of workers and passengers. The problem with leakage is especially likely in southern California because of the instability of the landscape.

To maintain structural integrity and human safety, rigorous earthquake design specifications are mandated in the construction of the subway tunnels. The original design specifications included minimal limits on the width of concrete used in the tunnel lining, the use of reinforcement materials for segments of tunnels that are thinner than specifications, and the installment of a sealed membrane lining to prevent water and gas leakage. The concrete tunnel liner was specified to be at least 12 inches thick, with extra rebar applied to thicknesses of less than 11 inches. The *Los Angeles Times*, after a review of inspection records and other public documents, reported that unfortunately radar testing by a consulting firm hired by the Metropolitan Transportation Authority (MTA) found that more than 2,000 feet of the subway tunnels under downtown Los Angeles are only 6 to 8 inches thick (*Las Vegas Review Journal* 1993b). The walls were less than 6 inches thick in two locations and less than 5 inches at one location, adjacent to the County Hall of Justice.

The safety of the Red Line tunnel walls and the necessary thickness of the walls have been subject to much debate. Tutor-Saliba Corporation, the company that built the tunnels in question, said that 6 inches of concrete are sufficient even with no reinforcement (*Las Vegas Review Journal* 1993b). Outside engineers, however, claim that tunnel walls less than 12 inches thick without the extra reinforcement would be more vulnerable to bending forces of an earthquake. The consequences of corrosive water and gas leakage have also been debated. Some groups assert that the poorly installed membrane allows for unnecessary seepage of gas and water in the tunnel and poses a serious health risk and a long-term threat to the structural integrity. Others note that some leakage is inevitable and can be monitored.

As a result of growing allegations of construction defects, a three-member panel of construction and engineering experts was selected by the MTA in September 1993 to evaluate the structural integrity of the Metro Red Line subway tunnels. The major conclusions of the review panel include the following (Cording, De Marco, and Hanson 1994:36–43):

- Concrete tunnel linings on the Metro Red Line are structurally adequate. They are, in their present condition, able to support the ground loads and accommodate the anticipated ground motions imposed by earthquakes.
- The tunnel lining will be able to support the ground loads and accommodate anticipated earthquake mo-

tions over the long term with regular maintenance and occasional repair.

- A detailed survey of the condition of the concrete tunnel lining revealed frequent cracks, some relatively wide, that appear to be caused largely by thermal effects and shrinkage.
- There is some potential, as leakage occurs, for corrosion of embedded reinforcement bars and the consequential spalling caused by that corrosion at construction joints. Observation needs to be continued over several seasons, and additional water samples should be taken.
- Deficiencies were found to be present and resulted in conditions that did not meet design requirements, such as minimum lining thickness and the addition of reinforcement in thin areas. Lining thickness and reinforcement conditions were evaluated, and results show that the lining is structurally adequate even though specified conditions were not met.
- Total water leakage in the tunnel is small, below the overall design limit.
- In view of the water leakage that has occurred, it is apparent that the high-density polyethylene (HDPE) membrane is breached in a number of locations.

The findings and work of the review panel, however, have been criticized on several grounds. Newspaper reports called into question the independence of the review panel, given that its chairman had worked for two years as a consultant to a major engineering firm that designed the subway tunnels (*Los Angeles Times* 1993). The integrity of the review has also been challenged because of public statements made by the panel chairman about the safety of the tunnel nearly three months before any testing was done. Other criticisms include (1) a secret clandestine tunnel grouting cover-up operation that was discovered by the *Los Angeles Times* just prior to the start of the review panel's investigation, (2) the failure of the panel to consult earthquake experts from the California Institute of Technology and seismologists from the U.S. Geological Survey, and (3) the panel's exclusion of information from a 125-page report by a senior inspector that identified and documented construction defects and apparent cover-ups. Although former engineers and construction workers have been extremely vocal about the quality and safety of the tunnel construction, time and nature will ultimately decide who is right in this ongoing controversy.

Allegations of misconduct on the Los Angeles Metro Rail construction project have been wide and varied. In a letter to Congressman John Dingell on March 31, 1992, Bob D'Amato, Mike Quint, and John Walsh (whistleblowers involved in the project) alleged that problems included:

- Widespread misuse of public funds
- Political corruption within local government agencies to cover up these problems
- Gross mismanagement of federal contracts requirements
- Bid-rigging by contract and governmental representatives
- Violations of federal Disadvantaged Business Enterprise (DBE)/Women Business Enterprise (WBE) regulations

- Violations of worker safety laws
- Insurance fraud and misuse of funds
- Violation of the Racketeering Influenced and Corrupt Organization Act (RICO)
- Illegal favoritism toward preferred contractors, including a conflict of interest with local governmental and state representatives
- Double billing by contractors for work that was already completed
- Installation of construction materials that did not meet the contract's requirements
- Falsified quality control reports that led directly to millions of dollars in construction cost overruns and the potential of injury to the future riding public

Mike Quint's Accusations About Construction Practices on the Red Line Tunnel

Mike Quint was a senior inspector on the construction of the Los Angeles Metro Rail project during the period October 1987 to April 1991. As a civil engineer, Quint has more than thirty years of construction management experience. Prior to his work on Metro Rail, he was an engineer on more than twenty separate projects throughout the states of California, Nevada, Alaska, and Texas and in Saudi Arabia.

Senior inspectors are the quality control agents in the construction industry. Their job entails reviewing field construction work for compliance with contract specifications and drawings. When construction practices are deemed unacceptable by senior inspectors, standard operating procedures in the industry require that (1) a noncompliance report be filed by the construction management firm, (2) a dollar amount be attached for the noncompliance condition, and (3) payment to the contractor be held back until the problem is fixed.

As a senior inspector, Quint reported to his supervisors and outside sources numerous accounts of deficiencies in the tunnel construction. According to written documents presented to the U.S. attorney general, Quint observed or had knowledge of the following concerns in the construction and management of the Red Line tunnel:

- Concrete pour items such as reinforcing steel and structural concrete were not being inspected properly. Quint gave repeated warnings to his supervisors about these problems in 1989 and 1990.
- Reinforcing steel rebar was missing at several locations.
- Approval was given to the contractor to form and pour incoming service hatch walls and then backfill the walls within twelve hours after the concrete pour. The limited time period was a gross violation of contract specifications and recognized national structural codes.
- Platform stairs were missing about 25 percent of the structural section and about 50 percent of the reinforcing steel. Quint considered these problems to be indicative of the pattern of faulty and sloppy inspection and a lack of respect for the contract drawings.
- Noncompliance reports were usually not written to track and ensure the correction of structural deficien-

cies, indicating a lack of control and the covering up of many critical defects.

- Specified procedures were not followed in the installation of the tunnel HDPE membrane. On several occasions the tunnel welders came into the work station without the required testing apparatus. Welders were not performing the "shear and peel" tests that measure the integrity of the weld.
- Night shift welders were not certified.
- Concrete specifications that require placement within ninety minutes and water/cement ratio requirements were not enforced.

Reporting Channels

Most persons who report fraud, waste, or abuse on the job begin with disclosing this information to higher-ranking employees within the organization and resort to external reporting only when these internal channels have been proven to be ineffective. As a whistleblower, Mike Quint reported his concerns about the falsification of inspection reports and the concealment of defects to officials within and outside the Metro Rail construction company.

As part of his job as senior inspector, Quint reported instances of shoddy construction and design defects to his supervisors. Their inaction after the receipt of many of his complaints, however, was a primary reason for his public disclosures of quality control problems. From early 1991 through 1997, Mike Quint remained incredibly persistent in reporting his concerns about construction defects to various city, state, and federal officials. A listing of the external

agents that Quint informed about defects and safety concerns, and the type of correspondence, includes in chrono-
logical order:

- Meeting with the Federal Bureau of Investigation
  (FBI) regarding defects and public safety
- Meeting with Fred Macksoud, deputy district attor-
  ney, County of Los Angeles, Environmental Crimes/
  OSHA Division
- Letter to Macksoud regarding defects and public
  safety issues in the Los Angeles tunnel
- Letter about quality control and public safety to
  Ralph Nader, consumer advocate
- Letter about public safety concerns sent to multiple
  members of the Los Angeles County Board of Super-
  visors (Antonovich, Dana, Edelman, Hahn, Molina);
  multiple members of the California State Assembly
  (Friedman, Hayden, Katz); Los Angeles City Council
  member Yaroslavsky; California senator Rosenthal;
  California governor Wilson; U.S. congressmen Mat-
  sui and Levine; Los Angeles mayor Bradley
- Letter to Macksoud outlining Quint's rebuttal com-
  ments to a report submitted by Rail Construction
  Corporation, a subsidiary of the Los Angeles County
  Transportation Commission
- Letter about defective construction to Hill Interna-
  tional, a watchdog group for the U.S. Department of
  Transportation
- Presentation on construction defects and public
  safety issues at a meeting of the Rail Construction
  Corporation

- Letter outlining major problems in the Metro Rail construction project to U.S. congressman Dingell
- Letter about defects and public safety to Chairman Antonovich of the Los Angeles County Board of Supervisors
- Presentation on defects and public safety at a California Transportation Commission Meeting
- Letter to Executive Director Peterson, Los Angeles County Transportation Commission
- Letter to Nick Patsaouras, Southern California Rapid Transit District
- Letter to Controller/Treasurer Rubin, Southern California Rapid Transit District
- Press conference/presentation with Los Angeles councilwoman Flores on construction defects
- Presentation on defects and public safety to the Los Angeles County Transportation Commission
- Letter about defects and public safety to Chairman Antonovich of the Los Angeles County Board of Supervisors
- Multiple presentations on defects and public safety to Los Angeles County Transportation Commission Safety Committee meetings
- Letter requesting construction documents to President McSpedon, Rail Construction Corporation
- Two-year follow-up letter about construction defects and cover-ups to Los Angeles County district attorney Garcetti, forwarded to Los Angeles County supervisors, Los Angeles City Council members, FBI, Chief Executive Officer White of the Los Angeles

County Metropolitan Transportation Authority, and
U.S. congressman Duncan
- Letter about construction defect cover-ups and pub-
lic health/safety issues to multiple parties, including
U.S. congressman Duncan and the U.S. Department
of Transportation, Office of Inspector General
- Letter to President Clinton
- Letter to Nevada senator Richard Bryan

In addition to this correspondence, extensive media coverage of construction costs and defects in the subway tunnels has been provided by the *Los Angeles Times*. Multiple
stories in this newspaper covered the allegations of Mike
Quint. When I asked Mike Quint what compelled or persuaded him to report the incidents of construction defect,
he said it was his professional duty as a licensed quality
control engineer and that there were serious public safety
concerns.

The U.S. Army Corps of Engineers in January 1996 issued
a report on the Metro Red Line tunnels that had been requested by the U.S. Department of Transportation's Office
of the Inspector General. This report is important because it
confirmed Mike Quint's original allegations that he had
presented to the U.S. attorney general and Los Angeles
County district attorney in June 1991. The report concluded
that safety and maintenance problems could develop
within five years and that "catastrophic failure," involving
public health and safety, could be avoided with adequate
periodic inspection and maintenance. The MTA panel report in February 1994 and the subsequent remedial work
provide additional independent validation of his claims.

Several aspects of Mike Quint's odyssey through various city, county, state, and federal agencies have immediate implications for other whistleblowers. First, efforts to identify and correct these problems have been severely impeded by officials' "passing of the buck" and a general diffusion of responsibility. Much of the correspondence between Quint and agencies includes specific references of the form "thank you, but this is not our problem or jurisdiction." A U.S. representative went so far as to claim that "congressional courtesy" dictated that the local California representative be informed about this problem before other elected officials outside California should deal with the complaint. This tendency to deflect responsibility for action will derail most attempts by whistleblowers to expose fraud, waste, and abuse. Second, the Quint case illustrates that persistence is often mandatory for exposing misconduct. It may take years for the original misconduct to be ultimately exposed and corrected. As of early 1998, Mike Quint remained in litigation about his disclosures of construction defects, a full eight years after his initial inquiries. Third, allegations of fraud, waste, or abuse are widely met with opposition and counterclaims. In the case of Mike Quint, both the management company and the construction firm have adamantly denied most of the allegations.

Consequences for the Whistleblower

The most obvious consequence of whistleblowing for Mike Quint involved his employment status. Quint contends that his abrupt transfer to another contract and his subsequent termination were a direct consequence of his efforts to maintain professional standards and expose misconduct in the construction process. The reporting of inadequate field preparation to his supervisor (which ultimately resulted in two additional days of corrective action and the waste of eight truckloads of concrete) was identified by Quint as the triggering incident that led to his removal from the project. Quint also believes that he was blacklisted from future construction jobs and remained unemployed for eighteen months because he was labeled as a troublemaker. Although the company's justification for termination was the proverbial "reduction in force" necessity, Quint would not be different from other whistleblowers if his termination from the project was a direct reprisal for speaking out about organizational practices.

There are additional consequences for whistleblowers besides job transfers and terminations. In Mike Quint's case, these consequences involved a number of factors associated with declines in the quality of life. When I asked what happened to him for reporting these incidents, Quint said that he received negative job performance evaluations, had work more closely monitored by supervisors, was criticized or avoided by co-workers, and was blacklisted from getting another job in his field. The psychological and interpersonal consequences of whistleblowing for Mike Quint also include increased depression and anxiety, decreases in physical health, greater feelings of isolation and powerlessness, greater distrust of others, and greater problems with family relations. Quint succinctly describes how the whistleblowing experience has affected his views about work:

> Management rewards and promotes employees who don't rock the boat and go along with their program. Two of my co-worker

inspectors were later promoted, while I was removed from the project.

It [the whistleblowing experience] has reduced my trust and faith in people and in our justice system, especially the L.A. County D.A.

I [now] expect less personal benefits from work, and perform my duties as directed, with fewer questions of decisions or procedures.

If given the opportunity to do things all over again, Quint said he would not have reported the misconduct. Given his strong personal and professional convictions, this acknowledgment that he would remain silent if he could turn back the clock is a vivid reminder of the devastating personal impact of whistleblowing.

The Aftermath of Whistleblowing and Its Effectiveness

Whistleblowing has lasting consequences for the whistleblower and the offending organization. For Mike Quint, it is clear that his experience as a whistleblower has left deep scars. His attitudes toward work and co-workers have been forever tainted, and he still remains involved in civil litigation against the construction management company under the California False Claims Act. As is true of others who report organizational misconduct, the label of whistleblower has become Mike Quint's "master status."

Although whistleblowing is crucial for exposing organizational misconduct, the fact remains that few whistleblowers are able to achieve major changes in organizational practices. This is the case because organizations have a vested interest in maintaining current practices and will go to incredible lengths to discredit and sabotage the claims of whistleblowers. The process of whistleblowing is also so devastating for most people that their anger, frustration, and limited experience and power prevent them from collecting the relevant documentation to prove their case and effectively articulating their concerns to the appropriate authority.

Contrary to the case with most whistleblowers, however, the efforts of Mike Quint to expose construction defects and cover-ups were remarkably successful in improving the quality of tunnel construction, saving taxpayers' money, and enhancing public safety. As a result of his accusations and tenacity, the following outcomes have occurred on the Metro Rail: (1) Quality control procedures have been improved to enhance public safety, (2) noncompliance regulations have been enforced, (3) the construction management company was removed from the project, and (4) the tunnel contractor performed eight months of remedial work on the tunnel liners, at no cost to taxpayers, to ensure public safety. Several individuals involved with the Los Angeles Metro Rail system have also been convicted of criminal activity and sentenced to prison as a result of the disclosures by other whistleblowers on this project.

Quint's effectiveness at triggering these changes is largely due to his commitment to maintaining professional standards and exposing abuses of them; his disclosure of this information to a wide range of city, state, and federal officials; and his extensive documentation and record keeping that helped validate his accusations. His efforts to change construction policy and practices have recently involved letters to President Clinton and Senator Richard

Bryan of Nevada, requesting their assistance in the enactment of federal legislation similar to the California Criminal Liability Act. Regardless of the success of these current legislative efforts, there is no doubt that the ultimate safety of the Metro Rail system has been greatly enhanced by the allegations and criticisms leveled by Mike Quint and other whistleblowers.

Trudi Lytle and
the Clark County Public School System

Parents have long been confronted with the grisly choice between public and private education for their children. The typical advantages of private schools (such as smaller classes, better instruction, higher-quality equipment) are offset by the financial expenses of private schooling. Public schools are clearly cheaper for parents, but the phrase "you get what you pay for" often describes the relative quality of education in these institutions. Clearly, the optimal solution for parents would be to achieve the quality of educational services often thought to characterize good private schools within the context of a public school. Such a situation occurred recently in the Clark County Public School District (CCSD) in Las Vegas, Nevada.

The CCSD is the tenth largest school system in the country. It is also one of the fastest growing, with more than thirteen thousand students added to CCSD each year. Nevada's expenditure for public education of $5,126 per student, however, ranks only thirty-fifth among all states and lags far behind the national average (*Statistical Abstracts of the United States* 1996). When the dramatic population growth in Las Vegas is coupled with the relatively low state support for education, it isn't surprising that the quality of public education is a major social problem in the city.

As is true of other public school systems, several programs are provided for students in CCSD with particular talents or potential. One of these initiatives, the Student Options for Academic Realization (SOAR) program, was a pilot program for gifted students in the Marion Earl Elementary School that was implemented in the 1991–1992 school year. Compared to other programs and classes within this school and throughout the district, SOAR students were given preferential treatment in class size and instructional funds. SOAR classes were capped at twenty students when other classes in the school had far higher student-teacher ratios. Computer equipment and school supplies (such as dictionaries, folders, and workbooks) were widely available to SOAR students but not for other students at Earl.

Although the claim that "regular" students were suffering as a result of the preferential treatment of SOAR students was a severe criticism of the program, the pilot program gained greater notoriety because of the composition of the classroom. Specifically, thirteen of the forty participants in the program's first year were children of school district staff members (*Las Vegas Review Journal* 1994e). Given disproportionate funding for SOAR and the overrepresentation of teachers' and principals' children within this program, critics have charged that district staff were receiving a largely private education for their children at the public's expense.

Trudi Lytle's Whistleblowing Experience

Trudi Lytle is an elementary school teacher with more than twenty years of teaching experience in the CCSD. She was a fourth-grade teacher at Marion Earl Elementary when the SOAR program was implemented. In March 1992, Lytle drafted and submitted a letter to all southern Nevada legislators that exposed the operation of the SOAR program. Parts of the letter were also published in a Las Vegas newspaper. The letter raised questions about the unequal student-faculty ratios across classes, the number of program participants who were children of district staff, and the prevalence of zone variances to allow particular students in other neighborhoods to participate in the SOAR program. Lytle's fourth-grade classroom at the time had thirty-three students and limited school supplies. She called the SOAR program a private school within a public school system (*Las Vegas Review Journal* 1994b).

The direct consequences of Lytle's disclosures are subject to alternative viewpoints. However, several observations can be gleaned from newspaper accounts, court documents, and interviews with this whistleblower:

- Trudi Lytle was transferred from her fourth-grade class at Earl Elementary in January 1993. She claims that the involuntary transfer was due to harassment in retaliation for her letter to state lawmakers and her federal lawsuit against the school district and her former principal. School officials, in contrast, argue that her transfer was not punishment but rather "for the good of the students" and an effort to boost low morale at the elementary school (*Las Vegas Review Journal* 1994b).
- Lytle was reprimanded twice by her principal prior to the transfer. The first reprimand involved her re-

fusal to turn in school keys before summer vacation. The second admonishment cited Lytle for trying to write a letter to parents, criticizing the SOAR program (*Las Vegas Review Journal* 1994c).

- Faculty and staff at Earl Elementary submitted a letter to Dr. Cram (superintendent of CCSD) in October 1992, alleging that Lytle was an argumentative staff member who created an emotional uproar and dissension in the school. Lytle's attorney claimed that these signatures were obtained through coercion and misrepresentation, orchestrated by the principal, SOAR teachers, and specialists who disliked his client.

- Lytle was offered teaching assignments at three other schools after her involuntary transfer. She refused these assignments, saying that she should have the freedom to speak up without facing retaliatory action (*Las Vegas Review Journal* 1994d).

- Lytle was removed from her fourth-grade teaching position during the middle of the school year. Twenty of the twenty-nine parents who were surveyed wanted Lytle to return to continue teaching their children as soon as possible. The superintendent of Clark County schools determined that she should not be returned to Earl Elementary. This decision was made "with the best interest of the students at the school in mind." As a sign of support for Lytle, fewer than half of her students showed up for class for the two days following her transfer (*Las Vegas Review Journal* 1993a).

- Lytle was unable to work after she was notified of her transfer in January 1993. Two physicians testified that Lytle was incapable of returning to work, as she was suffering from stress and high blood pressure. After a period of time and a court injunction, however, she returned to teaching at Earl Elementary.

Legal Action Against the School District

After being informed of the transfer, Trudi Lytle had to consider her options. One option was to accept the decision and meekly acquiesce. Alternatively, the teachers' union could have been contacted on behalf of Lytle to determine whether formal rules were violated. Instead of these two alternatives, Lytle consulted an attorney to become more fully aware of her legal protections. Efforts by her attorney to resolve this situation outside of court were unsuccessful.

Lytle filed a civil rights suit in October 1992 against the principal, administrators, and the CCSD for intentionally depriving her of substantive and procedural due process rights. Lytle noted in the formal complaint that she exercised her First Amendment rights by expressing her opinion about the SOAR program but was retaliated against by the principal through harassment, threats and discipline, and transfer for criticizing the program and filing a lawsuit against the defendants. The defendants, however, claimed that Lytle was transferred because she caused dissension and morale problems. Lytle's attorney argued that the retaliation against his client was also designed to send a message to other school district employees that the administration could not be questioned and to "shut up and go along with the program" (*Las Vegas Review Journal* 1994e). As a direct result of the retaliation, Lytle said that she had suffered extreme emotional distress, humiliation, and embarrassment, causing her to be temporarily disabled. In her federal lawsuit, Lytle asked the court for the following relief:

1. An injunction requiring the defendants to place her back at Earl Elementary School
2. Compensatory damages in the amount of $500,000
3. Special damages in the amount of $200,000
4. Punitive damages in the amount of $500,000
5. Other and further relief as the court might wish to entertain

A jury returned a verdict in favor of Trudi Lytle in July 1994. The jury found that "plaintiff's [Lytle's] protected speech regarding the SOAR program was a substantial or motivating factor in the defendants' decisions to take action against the plaintiff." She was awarded damages in the amount of $135,000. The school district filed a motion for a new trial in U.S. District Court, claiming that the jury ignored instructions that required proof "beyond a preponderance of doubt" that school administrators violated her constitutional right to free speech (*Las Vegas Sun* 1994). Despite strong opposition from the school administration, Lytle's request for injunctive relief to return to Earl Elementary was granted by the federal judge. School officials urged the judge to stop the reinstatement of Lytle, saying the move would bring about a "tense and hostile atmosphere" (*Las Vegas Review Journal* 1994f).

Although the court ordered the school district to reinstate Lytle to Earl Elementary, the judge retained the school's authority to assign teachers to particular classrooms. Upon

notification that she was assigned to teach two kindergarten classes, Lytle submitted an emergency motion to the
federal court to order the district to place her in her former
classroom as a fourth-grade teacher. However, the judge refused this motion.

Lytle's legal disputes with the school district have continued beyond the initial federal case. Her attorney argued in
the emergency motion that her placement in the kindergarten class appeared to be intentional harassment because
she had never taught kindergarten in her previous twenty
years and there was a new, vacant fourth-grade classroom
available for that school year (*Las Vegas Sun* 1994). Lytle
currently remains in litigation with the school district about
continued harassment at Earl Elementary. She has also filed
legal action against the school district for not providing
coverage of medical and retirement benefits during the
bridge time period in which she was unable to work.

Consequences of Whistleblowing

Trudi Lytle's criticism of the SOAR program has dramatically altered her life. The experience of being a whistleblower has affected her physical and psychological well-
being, her faith and trust in others, and her feelings of
isolation and powerlessness. She has been medically
treated for stress and high blood pressure, and the psychological wounds from being removed from her fourth-grade
class in the middle of the school year would be felt by anyone in that position. Although most Americans may believe
that co-workers would respect and support them for reporting illegal acts by their employer, Lytle feels that she

has received little support from co-workers. In fact, she said she was "shocked to find out that many of [my] co-workers had the attitude 'If I close my eyes, it doesn't exist.'" Her continued legal battles with the school district increasingly add to the label of whistleblower as her "master status." In other words, much of who Trudi Lytle is, and what she does, remains intricately tied to her initial allegations of abuse in the public school system.

When I asked how this experience has changed her views about management and work, Lytle made an extremely poignant comment:

> The CCSD knows that very few people have the money or emotional/physical stamina to fight them in a legal battle. Therefore, they blatantly ignore the Nevada Revised Statutes and/or the U.S. Constitution where a person's only recourse is a legal battle. Although the teacher's union is one of the most powerful in the state, their *only* goal is to elect people to political office and *not* teacher's rights. Hopefully, both organizations will do some rethinking of their goals as a result of my lawsuit.

The Aftermath of Whistleblowing and Its Effectiveness

The effectiveness of Trudi Lytle in changing organizational practices and improving the public school system in Clark County is subject to interpretation and one's perspective. The costs and benefits of her allegations are summarized below.

As a consequence of Lytle's criticism, the SOAR program was disbanded, and there is now a more equal distribution of students across classrooms within each school. Students with the highest academic ability—who would have previously been in SOAR—now attend a regular classroom but are given accelerated training for a short time period each day in another classroom through a program called GATE (Gifted and Talented Education). Parents of these gifted students are probably pleased that their children are receiving some advanced training in public school. However, parents of children in the regular classroom will probably be miffed because their children aren't receiving the same educational advantages. Although the names have changed and the amount of special training has diminished, the continued existence of special classrooms for bright students makes the school district still susceptible to allegations of "elitism" and of running private schools within a public school setting. Under these conditions, Lytle's public exposure of the SOAR program appears to have had little impact on the unequal distribution of educational services in this public school system.

The lasting contribution of Lytle's disclosures on the legal protection of teachers is largely unknown. For example, as a direct consequence of the Lytle litigation, the Clark County School Board developed and approved a whistleblowing policy to encourage employees to disclose improper school actions (*Las Vegas Review Journal* 1994h). This policy proposed the establishment of channels for reporting misconduct through a hearing officer and mandated that all cases would be reviewed by the School Board. However, it is unclear whether such policies are proactive steps in disclosing misconduct or simply alternative administrative strategies to limit the public disclosures of whistleblowers. Given Trudi Lytle's ordeal and the continued allegations of retaliation against her, it is unlikely that many observers of misconduct in this work setting would speak out even if there were specific protective policies for whistleblowers. Would you?

Finally, the teachers' union, like other unions, would appear to be an ideal outlet for voicing complaints and seeking corrective action for whistleblowers in this context. Union representatives in most organizations provide a buffer to assure that workers' rights are protected. Although Lytle is extremely cynical of the operation of her union, it remains unknown whether her experiences have subsequently altered the responsiveness of the union in protecting teachers' rights.

Toxic Waste Disposal in Area 51

The desert in southern Nevada is a harsh and brutal place. Temperatures far above 100 degrees are a daily occurrence in the long summer months, and it can get bone-chilling cold on some winter nights. Plant and animal life is sparse. Besides a few Joshua trees, stiff shrubs, small reptiles, and the occasional rodent, the desert landscape is void of life. Given this barren environment, it is little wonder that the federal government designated a large chunk of this area for atomic testing in the 1950s. Prior to the Limited Test Ban Treaty in 1963, banning atmospheric testing of nuclear weapons, more than one thousand nuclear tests were conducted at the Nevada Test Site. This facility remains in operation and covers more than 1,300 square miles of desert and mountainous terrain.

Segments of this desolate area north of Las Vegas have also become a common hangout for UFO (unidentified fly-

ing object) buffs. Located on Highway 375 (the so-called ex-
traterrestrial highway), the small town of Rachel, Nevada,
has become the "must-see" stop for UFO enthusiasts. Its
reputation developed from the widely publicized claims in
the late 1980s of a government physicist, Bob Lazar, who alleged that he had worked on a secret "flying saucer base"
near this town. He said that the U.S. military had in its pos-
session at least nine alien-built flying saucers and was
studying the craft in order to reproduce their technology
(Campbell 1993:3). His allegations, ironically, have been
difficult to either confirm or refute, but they have clearly fu-
eled the appetites of UFO trekkers. The supposed flying
saucer that was said to have crashed at Roswell, New Mexico, in the 1950s was allegedly taken to the Nevada Test Site
for full investigation (*The Observer* [London] 1996). A photo
history of UFO sightings is on display in the Little A "Le"
Inn, a Rachel tavern and hangout for UFO watchers.

Tales of alien spacecraft and abductions in this area have
become a popular theme in television programs and
movies. An episode of the television program *The X-Files*
used this geographical area as its major theme, and talk
show host Larry King had a two-hour special that was
broadcast from the perimeter of a military installation in
the area. More recently, the major story line from the block-
buster movie *Independence Day*, depicting conquest and an-
nihilation of humans by slime-infested, green aliens, was
based on the storage of the Roswell spacecraft on a restricted military base in this area.

Although media accounts of alien encounters are popular
fiction and mythology to most people, a 40,000-acre area of
Air Force property adjacent to the northeast corner of the

test site may provide an explanation for the UFO sightings. Namely, the UFOs reported by many observers are often the landing lights of supersonic spy planes and military airliners that transport workers and supplies to a top-secret Air Force base (Campbell 1993). This facility has received growing public attention because of allegations of environmental crimes against its workers.

Groom Lake and Area 51

Even the name of this base is shrouded in controversy. It is often called Groom Lake because of its location on a dry lake bed, but locals call it Dreamland, Watertown, the Ranch, the Box, and the Pig Farm (*Popular Science* 1994; *Washington Post* 1997). Most of the geographical area of Groom Lake is contained in a sector of the Nevada Test Site dubbed Area 51, which apparently was its designation on old grid maps of the test site. Area 51 is the most common name for this military base. Officially, however, the base doesn't exist. Government maps show only a dry lake bed on the northeast corner of the Nevada Test Site. Military officials for years would neither confirm nor deny that the base even existed, but they now acknowledge that some activities take place in the area. The term "a remote test facility" is the only way the base can be described within the armed forces (*Popular Science* 1994:53). The Air Force's official position is that "there is an operating location near Groom Dry Lake," but the base has no name. Everything about Area 51 is classified; specific activities at the base in the past and present cannot be discussed (*Washington Post* 1997:F4).

By all accounts, however, Area 51 is the military's worst-kept secret. UFO enthusiasts and aircraft buffs have long ventured to the perimeter of the base to catch a glimpse or take photographs of various sightings. Before prime viewing areas (such as the so-called Freedom Ridge) surrounding Groom Lake were closed to public access in 1995, the activities at Area 51 were routinely monitored by a small cadre of civilians perched atop nearby mountains. Six-mile-long runways, aircraft hangars, radar towers, and many of the two hundred buildings could be seen by anyone who looked (*Wall Street Journal* 1996). Despite the best efforts at concealment, Russian satellites have photographed the base. Local residents in Las Vegas, about 120 miles southeast of the site, are fully aware of the existence of this top-secret base. Many of their neighbors are employed there, leaving for work early in the morning hours and supposedly having jobs at other locations. Observers on ridges surrounding Groom Lake who count daily air shuttles calculate that 1,500 to 2,500 people work at the base (*Popular Science* 1994:57). Others estimate that 1,000 civilians and 2,000 military personnel are employed at Area 51 (*Wall Street Journal* 1996).

For those who have visited the perimeter of Area 51, the surrounding area is an incredibly ominous sight. Metal signs warn trespassers that this is a Restricted Area, covered by military law. The perimeter signs also state: "Use of Deadly Force Authorized." High-powered, telemetry satellite dishes distort photographic images from unauthorized viewers, and solar-powered cameras monitor persons and objects approaching the perimeter. Motion sensors are set up along dirt roads, Jeep-driving security officers widely patrol the area, and helicopters or high-speed aircraft buzz intruders. The overall level of security in the area and the quick deployment of security agents make it blatantly obvious that this is a restricted area and visitors are not welcome.

Given that everything and everyone connected with Area 51 is classified, it is impossible to determine with certainty what goes on there. Nonetheless, most journalistic accounts provide a historical summary of the aircraft testing conducted at this base. For example, a feature article in *Popular Science* described the base's flight testing history in the following way:

> Groom Lake's role as a secret air base began in 1954, when the CIA gave Lockheed a contract to develop a spyplane that could fly higher than any aircraft yet built. The Soviet Union was to be the U-2's primary target. Lockheed test pilot Tony LeViter who had made the first flight in the hot F-104 fighter from which the U-2 was derived, was dispatched to find a location where tests of the slender-winged craft could be kept hidden. Flight testing of the Air Force SR-71 Spyplane and its predecessors, the CIA's A-12, was conducted there in 1962. Covertly obtained Soviet fighters were also hidden and flight-tested there. And about 10 years ago, the F-117A first flew at Groom Lake. During the 1980s an even faster replacement for the SR-71 appears to have begun flying out of Groom Lake—various reports have dubbed it Aurora, Senior Citizen, or Senior Smart—despite what the Air Force says to the contrary. Other secret projects likely to have been tested in recent years at Groom Lake include stealthy vertical-landing aircraft designed to covertly transport small groups of special-forces troops inside foreign territory. Recent years have brought even more growth. Construction of a parallel runway estimated to be 15,000 feet long was begun around 1989 to permit continued flight testing when winter flooding makes the main runway's northern half unusable. (1994:84)

Open-Pit Burnings and Exposure of
Workers to Toxic Smoke

The security surrounding personnel and activities at classified facilities like Area 51 extends to the destruction of old materials and chemicals. Garbage disposal at restricted areas in a world of high technology and intelligence must be handled with extreme care because even the most minute traces of fibers and chemicals, if placed in the wrong hands, may be sufficient to unravel the mysteries of the composition of secret weapons and radar-busting planes. Under this "mosaic theory" (see *Washington Post* 1997; *Wall Street Journal* 1996), the mere knowledge of particular materials or chemicals used at restricted facilities may be enough for a foreign enemy to figure out military operations and capabilities.

Although knowledge of the specific procedures for waste disposal at Groom Lake is restricted and under investigation by state and federal agencies, a group of former workers and their widows have alleged in federal lawsuits that open-pit burning of materials and chemicals was a routine occurrence throughout the 1980s. According to worker accounts, military officials armed with M-16s stood guard as truckloads of toxic waste, such as resins, paints, and solvents in 55-gallon drums, and other materials, such as computers, were covered with combustible materials, doused with jet fuel, and set ablaze in 100-yard-long by 25-foot-wide pits (see *Washington Post* 1997; *Wall Street Journal* 1996; *Las Vegas Sun*, 1996). The workers further alleged that the burnings occurred on a weekly basis and that some men had to go into the huge pits after the ashes cooled to ensure complete incineration of the materials. Workers in the pits and other employees downwind from the thick, choking clouds of poisonous smoke were said to be widely exposed to dioxins and furans from inhaling this toxic waste (*Washington Post* 1997; *Las Vegas Review Journal* 1993c).

One of the workers said to have been exposed to the burning toxic materials was Robert Frost. Frost was a sheet metal worker who constructed hangars and other buildings at Area 51. During the spring of 1988, Frost became so ill that he missed a week of work and applied for workers' compensation for lost wages. He told state hearing officers that one day while working atop a building his hands and neck turned red, and his face split open and began bleeding (*Las Vegas Review Journal* 1993c:3A). His employer fought the award for compensation, but Frost died in November 1989 before the appeal hearing was held. Two years later, the Frost compensation was ultimately denied after a company superintendent testified that no burning ever occurred at Area 51 (*Washington Post* 1997:F7).

After the death of her husband, Helen Frost filed a wrongful death lawsuit against Lockheed Corporation in 1993. An affidavit filed in the case by a biochemist said Frost's tissue samples revealed levels of dioxins from "substantial exposure to chemicals which contain and/or convert to dioxins and dibenzofurans" (*Las Vegas Review Journal* 1993d:1B). His dioxin levels were far in excess of persons living in an industrial environment. However, a U.S. District Court judge denied the widow's complaint in July 1993 on the grounds that the evidence linking Frost's death to dioxin exposure was inconclusive and insufficient to overcome Lockheed's claim that his death from liver disease was caused by excessive alcohol abuse (*Las Vegas Review Journal* 1993d:3A).

According to media accounts, Helen Frost was so convinced that Lockheed and the Air Force were trying to cover up the open-pit burning that she distributed flyers at union meetings and at bus stops, urging other Area 51 workers to get tested for dioxin exposure (*Las Vegas Review Journal* 1993d:3A). Based on her efforts, several additional events have transpired. First, more than ten workers have come forth anonymously to confirm the burning of toxic materials in open pits near Groom Lake (*Las Vegas Review Journal* 1993e:2B). Air Force officials neither confirm nor deny these allegations of toxic waste burnings from the Stealth aircraft project. Second, Helen Frost has compiled a list of more than twenty workers on the Stealth project at the facility who have either died or developed skin, kidney, liver, or heart problems (*Las Vegas Review Journal* 1993c:3A). Third, the state of Nevada's Environmental Protection Division has initiated an investigation for evidence of open-pit burning at Groom Lake. Fourth, Helen Frost contacted the Project on Government Oversight, a nonprofit government watchdog group, which began an investigation of her accusations. Jonathan Turley, a George Washington University law professor and director of the pro bono Environmental Law Advocacy Center, has subsequently provided legal representation for Helen Frost and more than twenty-five workers at no charge.

Lawsuits Involving Environmental Crimes

Jonathan Turley has filed two lawsuits on behalf of Helen Frost and six workers. The lawsuits are directed at disclosing environmental crimes at Groom Lake and seeking criminal prosecution for those who committed them. The suits also seek medical monitoring and possible compensation for those who were injured (*Las Vegas Review Journal* 1994a:1B). Turley says that he can prove the government violated the Resource Conservation and Recovery Act, the federal law regulating hazardous waste (*Wall Street Journal* 1996:4A). Burning hazardous waste in open trenches is a crime punishable by up to fifteen years in prison and a $1 million fine.

One federal lawsuit was filed against the Environmental Protection Agency (EPA) in August 1994 to compel that agency to test the contaminated area at Area 51 and report the findings publicly (George Washington University 1994). The second lawsuit during that time period named Secretary of Defense William Perry, National Security Advisor Anthony Lake, and Air Force Secretary Sheila Widnall for violating hazardous waste laws at the secret Groom Lake base (*Las Vegas Review Journal* 1994g:4B). The charges involved violations of the federal facility reporting and inventory requirements, violations of the ban on open burning of hazardous waste used to build the Stealth fighter, illegal land disposal of hazardous waste, and illegal trucking of hazardous materials (Project on Government Oversight 1994).

Efforts by whistleblowers to press legal action against federal agencies for environmental crimes at Area 51 have been hampered by several major impediments to evidence collection and disclosure. First, everything and everyone connected to the base are classified, so employees cannot talk about the work they do or have seen. In fact, Area 51 workers face ten years in prison if they are caught disclosing anything about their jobs (*Washington Post* 1997:F4). Second, the official government position is that Area 51 does not exist, requiring attorneys to prove its existence in the absence of classified documents. Third, collaborating witnesses are unwilling to come forward to testify because of fear of government reprisals. Turley believes that the Air Force's Office of Special Investigations is trying to photograph or otherwise hunt down the John Doe plaintiffs in the lawsuits in order to bring charges against them for breaching national security (*Washington Post* 1997:F4). Fourth, the government's unwillingness to grant complete immunity for all crimes the workers may have committed or for all unauthorized disclosures of classified information also severely impedes the success of litigation. Under these conditions, it is little wonder that efforts to expose environmental crimes and personal injuries at the classified facility have been met with great opposition.

The government's primary defense in the allegations of environmental crime has been national security. Government lawyers have been adamant that any disclosures of the type of materials burned at Area 51, or even the acknowledgment of the very existence of the base, may compromise national safety and jeopardize military operations. In fact, Justice Department lawyers even went so far as to invoke the military—and state—secrets privilege *before* any evidence had been presented that could be challenged on the grounds it needed protection for national security reasons (*Las Vegas Review Journal* 1994i:2B). The lawsuits filed by the whistleblowers did not contest the government's need for national security but contended that the shroud of secrecy had been used to hide hazardous waste violations and other environmental crimes. Jonathan Turley has been quoted as saying that "this case has little to do with national security and a great deal to do with accountability within the government system" (*Wall Street Journal* 1995:B3).

The original lawsuits brought by the whistleblowers have been dismissed in federal court. U.S. District Court judge Philip Pro in March 1996 dismissed the lawsuit brought by former workers against the Air Force on the grounds that national security at Groom Lake must take priority over the alleged health and environmental damages (*Las Vegas Sun* 1996b). Given the restrictions placed on evidence because of national security, the judge concluded that no controversy could be shown and a lawsuit could not be brought to the court because no information on the actual location of the alleged offenses was available to the workers. The lawsuit against the EPA was also dismissed by a federal judge, who said it fell outside his jurisdiction because President Clinton had given a presidential exemption and signed an order to keep Groom Lake work conditions a secret (*Las Vegas Sun* 1996a). Turley has appealed the dismissals of the lawsuits on behalf of his clients. In fact, as of September 1997, there were seven separate appeals under court review that derived from these lawsuits against the government and its agencies.

Four months after the suits were filed in August 1994, the EPA launched an investigation of the alleged environmental crimes at Area 51. More than two years later, government prosecutors were attempting to get permission to interview one of the John Doe workers who was said to have witnessed these violations. Although this action might validate the workers' claims, the whistleblowers' attorney, Jonathan Turley, thinks the criminal investigation of environmental violations is designed primarily to compile information for purposes of criminal and civil reprisals against his clients (*Las Vegas Sun* 1996c).

Issues for Other Whistleblowers

The experiences of Helen Frost and the John Doe workers illustrate several problematic aspects of whistleblowing. First, these workers are faced with a clear no-win situation. If they report violations to prevent future harm to themselves, other workers, and the public, they dramatically increase their risks of serious civil and criminal sanctions for violating national security. In contrast, if they do nothing, they risk further physical injuries to themselves and the environment. Second, there are nearly insurmountable obstacles for whistleblowing in cases involving government agencies: (1) Persons often do not have legal standing to take action against the government; (2) government officials can block access to supporting evidence through executive privilege, national security, and other avenues; and (3) government agencies have a far wider array of legal defense staff at their disposal than does the typical whistleblower. Third, as seen with other whistleblowers, legal action is often a high-risk and low-reward activity that is prohibitive in both its financial costs and time. Helen Frost, for example, has been involved in litigation on behalf of her husband since 1988 without successful resolution. If not for the efforts of such pro bono watchdog organizations as the

Government Oversight Project and Jonathan Turley's Environmental Crimes Project, the whistleblowers at Area 51 would have been severely restricted in their legal recourse.

The Aftermath of Whistleblowing and Its Effectiveness

Although the original lawsuits by the whistleblowers were dismissed and their appeals are still pending in federal court, their actions have had several meaningful implications for increasing public awareness and future military and government activities. First, the whistleblowers' lawsuits set a precedent as the first time actions against a "black-budget" facility had gone to court. Prior to their efforts, workers at such facilities were told that they could not retain a lawyer or file federal action (*Las Vegas Review Journal* 1996). Second, the government was forced to perform an inspection of environmental violations and a complete inventory of disposal practices on its own facility, weakening the near immunity of government activity to public scrutiny. Third, the lawsuits raised serious questions about the blanket defense of "national security" and increased public awareness of the potential abuses of this defense. Fourth, greater safety precautions have probably been taken in the disposal of toxic materials at classified facilities, reducing the health risk to workers and the environment. Fifth, the treatment of workers in the Area 51 case reveals a particular hypocrisy in presidential policies. Specifically, President Clinton made a public apology in 1995 to the victims of secret radiation tests in New Mexico, saying that when the government does wrong there is a moral responsibility to admit it. A few days before that speech, however, Clinton had signed an executive order that exempted Area 51 from disclosing its pollution records and ultimately any evidence of toxic poisoning of the workers (*Wall Street Journal* 1996).

As for remedies or benefits for the whistleblowers, it appears that their plight has changed very little as a result of their actions. The government has not, as of yet, acknowledged that their injuries were directly caused by environmental crimes, and they have not received any additional federal assistance in their medical treatment for exposure to toxic materials. Unfortunately, the fate of the workers at Area 51 seems remarkably similar to nuclear test site employees, uranium miners, and "downwinders" exposed to radiation from atomic bomb testing. Like the workers at Area 51, many of these workers and citizens got sick and died, but the courts have not held anyone responsible for their suffering (*Washington Post* 1997).

Norm Buske and
the Puget Sound Naval Shipyard[1]

Oceanographer Norm Buske makes people nervous. He was barred from French Polynesia after investigating nuclear military projects in the area. He raised eyebrows in Washington State when he sent then governor Booth Gardner a jar of radioactive mulberry jelly made from fruit picked on the edge of the Hanford Nuclear Reservation.

---

1. This section is reprinted with permission from Government Accountability Project, "Whistleblower of the Month," 1997. Available: http://www.accessone.com/gap.

More recently, the U.S. Navy has decided Buske is a hazard to operations at the Puget Sound Naval Shipyard (PSNS) in Washington State.

For years, Norm Buske held a job as an investigator of car accidents and fires. Then in 1985, he traded in his corporate suit and tie for a wet suit and made monitoring radioactive waste at nuclear military sites his primary activity. The Government Accountability Project (GAP) is defending Buske in his efforts to investigate contamination in Puget Sound, where the U.S. Navy decommissions old nuclear ships.

With advanced degrees in oceanography and physics from Johns Hopkins University and the University of Connecticut, Buske is a serious scientist. He is also a serious environmental activist, dedicated to the proposition that citizens have a right to know—and to verify—what their government is up to, particularly when public health and environmental safety are at risk. Since 1993, Buske has used funds from his own pocket to collect biological samples from ten Navy facilities throughout the country. His aim is to test marine life for signs of radiation that may have escaped from the Navy's nuclear-propelled ship engines.

The only shipyard in the United States that flunked his initial screening was the PSNS. Buske has twice produced reports documenting his findings of low levels of radiation there. The Navy counters that it has never leaked any measurable amounts of radiation into the ocean waters surrounding the shipyard.

Buske began to conduct research near the naval station by gathering samples of kelp (and other algae that filter radioactive material) in Puget Sound's Sinclair Inlet, known as Restricted Area 2 (RA2) because of its proximity to the naval station. To comply with existing military regulations barring ships from the area, Buske did not boat into RA2. Instead he swam into the inlet from a nearby vessel. Buske frequently notified Navy personnel in advance of his investigative dives. On occasion, the Navy escorted the scientist and used his samples for their own research.

This tolerant attitude evaporated, however, after Buske published test results that revealed trace amounts of cadmium 109 in the naval shipyard. This report conflicted with the Navy's Blue Book, the department's annual monitoring report of radioactivity test results.

Buske's findings triggered a joint study by the EPA and the state Department of Health in January 1994. Although the study did not confirm the presence of cadmium 109, officials did find iodine 131—a nuclear fission product linked to cancer—in the Sinclair Inlet. Scientists argued that the levels detected were low enough to be essentially harmless. And government officials pointed out that it is unclear whether the iodine comes from a nearby city sewer outfall or from the shipyard.

These arguments, Buske insisted, missed the point: What is at issue is the reliability of the Navy's radioactive-testing systems. "All along, the Navy has said, 'Trust us, we're monitoring ourselves, and we're not finding anything,'" he said. "Now we find radioactivity right in the middle of the shipyard. Why didn't they find it? It shows us either the Navy's self-monitoring is not good, or they're not telling us everything." Buske was convinced that further research was necessary to determine the source and extent of the problem. The Navy, however, refused to grant his requests to take samples closer to the shipyard's operations.

Buske continued to gather samples from the restricted area. On September 22, 1994, he was joined by friends from Greenpeace, who escorted him on an inflatable raft to the perimeters of RA2. As usual, Buske had informed the Navy of his plans. He and his friends were met by Navy and Coast Guard patrol boats that remained on the scene while Buske completed his dive.

His first swim was successful, and he returned to the raft with a sample. On his second attempt the Navy moved to detain him. The Coast Guard forcibly towed the Greenpeace vessel into the restricted area: The boat and its crew were then seized for violating the prohibited access order. Buske's samples were thrown overboard, and he was issued a letter barring him from the shipyard.

Acting on the belief that the restricted area was not part of the PSNS, Buske swam in to collect more samples a few days later. This time he was arrested and taken in his wet suit to the federal courthouse in Seattle. Buske's case came before Judge William L. Dwyer on May 23, 1995.

The judge found him not guilty. RA2 was not part of PSNS, Dwyer ruled, and the restricted area policy did not exclude civilian swimmers, only boats or rafts. What's more, the judge decided, oceanographer Norm Buske was not a threat to national security. The next day, Buske returned to the restricted area with his wet suit and sample containers.

But the Navy was gearing up to block Buske. Patrols were increased, and the Navy requested that the local Coast Guard publish an emergency rule barring civilian swimmers from the area. Navy officials contended that the emergency rule was implemented simply to close a loophole in their security net and increase civilian safety. They said that standard operating procedures made RA2 a dangerous place for swimmers. In a letter dated May 26, 1995—one day after Dwyer's ruling—Commander V. T. Williams of PSNS stated: "The crew of an operating warship is authorized, in some cases, to shoot to kill swimmers approaching it."

The Navy also claimed that Buske's activities were costing them too much money. Navy spokesperson John Gordon said that each of Buske's dives cost the department between $15,000 and $20,000 in personnel and legal costs. Buske countered that most of these costs have gone into efforts to prosecute him.

In June 1995, GAP asked a federal court for a preliminary injunction to stop enforcement of the emergency rule. GAP attorney Sarah Levitt and General Counsel Bob Seldon argued that Buske's First Amendment right to gather information was violated by the Navy's action. "There is no independent accountability or oversight of Navy activities," Levitt said. "Norman Buske was effectively censored for trying to provide it." The suit forced the Navy to invite the EPA and the Washington State Department of Health for an independent inspection of the restricted area, which was conducted with behind-the-scenes assistance from Buske. Three months later, these tests confirmed trace amounts of iodine 131 in the naval shipyard.

The Navy moved quickly to further prohibit public access to the restricted area. In August 1995, an "interim final rule" went into effect making it illegal for civilian swimmers to use the waters around the PSNS. The new restriction was implemented without a time for public notice or comment. This was an extreme measure, Levitt observed. "Temporarily dispensing with notice and comment is permitted under the law but only in an emergency situation. There was no emergency here except for the threat of the public learning the truth through Buske's activities, and the fact remains that the government did not allow opportunity for citizens to voice concern over this sudden change in policy until after the rule was in effect." Buske, meanwhile, called the emergency ruling an "unconstitutional sham" designed to stop the Navy from being accountable to the public.

On September 11, 1995, Buske dove again into the restricted area without permission for access. He was detained by Navy personnel who informed him that any subsequent trespasses would result in arrest. Later that day, Buske returned to the restricted area and was arrested before he could collect any samples. GAP General Counsel Bob Seldon said, "In keeping with the time-honored principles of civil disobedience, Norm Buske has contested immoral government activity honestly and forthrightly. He has done so not for personal gain or for notoriety but in service to his fellow citizens."

With Buske awaiting trial, GAP joined him as a plaintiff and filed a second complaint challenging the government's interim rule and forcing it to publish a final rule. GAP again argued that Buske's First Amendment right to gather information was violated by the military's actions. The day before Buske's trial, GAP asked for a second preliminary injunction. Before GAP could make its case, however, the government moved to make the rule final. Buske's second trial was also before Judge Dwyer. On January 23, 1996, Buske was found guilty of trespassing on federal property and fined $100. An anonymous donor readily made the payment.

Buske continues to work on exposing radioactive contamination in and around the PSNS. He now operates a regular monitoring station next to RA2. On March 4, 1996, Navy officials confirmed an informant's story to a local newspaper that the USS *Arkansas* leaked radioactive materials at the shipyard. Buske's request for access into the naval shipyard to examine the size of the leak was denied without explanation.

Buske remains undaunted. "I know I'm just one person against the entire Navy, and my message can be easy to ignore," he has said. "But what I want is simple. I want them to hear us say, 'Wait a minute! We live here and don't want you accidentally dumping things, and then lying about it.' We want them to be honest and, most important, to treat us with dignity. Our humanity is on the line."

Mark O'Neal and the Nation's Nuclear Bomb Factory[2]

The Department of Energy's Pantex plant is located deep in the Texas panhandle. It is there that the nation's nuclear stockpile was assembled during the Cold War years. And it is there that these nuclear weapons are being disassembled today, bomb by bomb: Over 50,000 warheads have been dismantled to date [1997]. The risks are enormous. An acci-

---

2. This section is reprinted with permission from Government Accountability Project, "Whistleblower of the Month," 1997. Available: http://www.accessone.com/gap.

dental detonation of the high explosives components of a single weapon could mean the spread of deadly radioactive materials—a grave threat to public health and the environment. Pantex claims that it takes this responsibility very seriously. "The top priority at Pantex," according to a promotional pamphlet, "is the safety and health of its workers and the public, and the protection of the environment." Many of the workers at the plant disagree. Among them is GAP whistleblower Mark O'Neal.

For fifteen years, O'Neal worked on the line at Pantex as a highly regarded production technician. Plant supervisors, according to O'Neal, "were always stressing production, never safety. They even had competitions for line workers and awarded beers for the highest production. Weapons were often handled without a 'buddy.' Paper clips were used in place of locking pins in the machinery used to roll nuclear weapons through hallways. Tape was used to cover holes in task exhausts used during tritium operations. The highest priority was production. Everything else, including safety, ranked below."

From the time of his first assignment in mid-1980, O'Neal routinely observed such health and safety violations. He reported them diligently to the management of Mason & Hanger, Silas-Mason Co., Inc., the contractor that operates Pantex on behalf of the federal government. Just as routinely, O'Neal says, Mason & Hanger ignored these violations, often ordering workers to continue working in the face of known hazards. In the summer of 1994, O'Neal raised concerns about safety problems caused by a belligerent and irresponsible co-worker who repeatedly threatened other workers with physical violence.

In October 1994, O'Neal filed a retaliation complaint against his employer with the Department of Energy's Office of Contractor Employee Protection. On July 19, 1996, O'Neal and Mason & Hanger reached a mutually agreeable settlement.

Among the allegations reported by O'Neal and other workers to GAP were:

- nuclear weapons stored in bays not equipped for storage, thus exposing employees to radiation
- weapons parts leaving work bays without proper identification regarding possible radiation hazards
- bolts missing from covers of hoists used to lift and position weapons
- workers instructed to continue working when tritium alarms sounded
- intentional interference with airborne radioactivity monitors

Problems at Pantex date back years. The silence about conditions at the plant, however, is not surprising. Pantex is an imposing 16,000-acre facility located 17 miles northeast of the small town of Amarillo in the Texas high plains. Pantex has been the center of life in Amarillo for decades—first as a bomb plant in the early days of World War II and then as a nuclear weapons production and disassembly plant beginning in the 1950s. With a workforce of thirty-eight hundred, Pantex is the business of Amarillo today. Under such conditions—and particularly in economic hard times—few workers have been inclined to question operations at the plant.

Pantex management, for its part, has done little to encourage openness about health and safety concerns. Threats are common currency at the plant. According to workers, management issued constant threats that the plant would shut down if they did not get the work out. They were told that management would close the plant if workers did not buy in. On the job, workers who expressed concerns were often relocated to other work stations and replaced with more compliant employees. In one case, a supervisor who had misplaced weapons parts owing to rushed and sloppy operations enjoined his workers to assist him in covering up the incident. Later, at a pre-shift meeting, the supervisor said ominously that he had discovered a rat in his group and that they should take care of the problem "out at the railroad tracks."

Given the long-standing atmosphere of fear and distrust at the plant and in Amarillo, GAP attorneys were astounded at the local response to GAP's investigation into Pantex. In August [1996], GAP sent an investigative team of attorneys—Tom Carpenter, Bob Seldon, and Joanne Royce—to interview workers and verify O'Neal's whistleblower disclosures. More than a dozen current and former co-workers and line supervisors at the plant came forward to validate O'Neal's allegations and concerns and to add some of their own.

The health problems reported by plant workers suggest that safety violations at the plant were taking a heavy toll. One Amarillo resident reported to GAP that her husband, a former Pantex employee, died of pancreatic cancer nine days after his doctor told him he could return to work. A female employee assigned to the unloading dock in the middle of her pregnancy delivered a child born with no feet or fingers. Toolmaker John Bell has been in and out of surgery ten times for illnesses related to radiation sickness, including degenerative nerve disease, hypothyroidism, and chronic fatigue. Bell says that his health has steadily declined after he performed a task without receiving safety instructions from the cell supervisor: It took him a year of persistent inquiry to discover that he had been exposed to uranium contamination.

To make matters worse for employees suffering from job-related health problems, Pantex's intimidating presence in Amarillo has led many local doctors to refuse to treat plant workers. One of the first line workers at the plant told GAP about the autoimmune deficiency disease she contracted, diagnosed by her doctor as caused by overexposure to nuclear radiation. Following his diagnosis, the doctor received a letter from Pantex management demanding that he "explain" that his patient's illness had nothing to do with conditions at the plant. The doctor said he would comply if Pantex shared the patient's on-the-job medical file with him. Pantex refused. The worker has since been told that some of her records are inexplicably missing or unaccounted for. She is soon to be unemployed without benefits because Pantex doctors claim her illness is not work related. John Bell, meanwhile, has been fighting unsuccessfully to receive workers' compensation from Pantex since he was forced to quit working for health reasons. With the help of a local nonprofit environmental watchdog group, Safe Texans Against Nuclear Disposal (STAND)— which filed for information on the case under the Freedom of Information Act—Bell discovered that the company had paid off doctors and other witnesses to the tune of $300,000 to win the case against him. Bell was seeking only $87,000 in workers' compensation.

GAP attorneys have heard not only from workers and their families but also from concerned residents in the Amarillo area who have noticed trends in health problems that they believe are related to operations at Pantex. Jeri and James Osborne, who live northeast of Pantex in nearby Carson County, began marking a map with pins to indicate the homes of neighbors who have died of cancer. To date, the map is marked with more than two hundred pins. "I can't say there's any sure connection," Jeri said, "but it does look kind of suspicious."

Together with O'Neal and other concerned workers and residents, GAP is seeking to document and demand action from Pantex on the pattern of abuses. "Our goal is to make the plant safer for the twenty-first century," explained Seldon. "Pantex workers and the community deserve that. It's time to end the Cold War–era approach to bomb-making in which weapons producers demanded secrecy and loyalty from their plants, but not accountability."

Dr. Jeffrey Wigand and the Tobacco Industry

The tobacco industry has been attacked on a variety of fronts over the last two decades. These antitobacco activities include bans on cigarette advertisements on television, warning labels from the surgeon general on cigarette packages, no-smoking ordinances applying to public places, reports on the medical consequences of secondhand smoke, assertions that the "Joe Camel" character entices smoking among teenagers, and periodic crackdowns on convenience

stores for selling cigarettes to minors. Throughout these attacks, the tobacco industry has remained steadfast in its denial that smoking is harmful and that nicotine is an addictive drug. Industry officials, lawyers, and scientists have
widely criticized evidence from independent sources of the
dangers of tobacco and estimates that more than 425,000
people die every year from smoking cigarettes. Claims of
dubious corporate practices within the tobacco industry,
however, escalated dramatically with the public dissemina-
tion by Merrell Williams of secret industry documents.

As a paralegal for a Louisville law firm between 1989 and
1992, Merrell Williams worked in the document room at
Brown and Williamson Tobacco Corporation (B&W), coding
internal reports and research findings presumably to help
people suing the tobacco industry should the records come
out in court (*Courier-Journal* [Louisville, Kentucky] 1997). It
became apparent to Williams, however, that the primary
purpose of the internal coding system was to conceal evidence and internal records. He secretly copied about four
thousand pages of these B&W documents and released them
to antitobacco advocates. According to newspaper accounts,
these documents revealed to the public the following information about practices within the tobacco company:

- B&W general counsel told the company in 1963 that
  it was in the business of selling an addictive drug,
  and its research scientists have reported for years
  that the product can pose serious health risks for
  users.
- Scientists conducted a program breeding high-
  nicotine plants, and B&W used that tobacco in sev-

eral brands. The company studied the relationship between "nicotine dose" and "smoker satisfaction." The company said this was all about flavor, but David Kessler, who was then the Food and Drug Administration (FDA) commissioner, testified before Congress that the tobacco industry manipulated nicotine levels to keep smokers addicted.

- Although denying that cigarettes were harmful, B&W worked privately to develop a safe cigarette. When it became apparent that it was not going to achieve a safe cigarette, it intensified efforts to counter the evidence that cigarettes are dangerous.
- B&W identified secondhand smoke as a health issue almost a decade before the government or independent scientists did, but it did not share the information publicly.
- B&W denied marketing cigarettes to young people— yet it viewed educational programs to prevent young nonsmokers from taking up the practice as a threat to the industry; it viewed legislation to curb smoking among children as a negative development for the industry; it took notice that higher cigarette taxes might price cigarettes out of the reach of young people; it bought onscreen advertisements in movie theaters and paid to have its brands scripted into movies.
- B&W set up special procedures for company lawyers to review scientific research documents so the company could claim attorney-client privilege and withhold the information when plaintiffs tried to seek it. (*Courier-Journal* 1997)

The tobacco company has accused Williams in lawsuits of stealing the documents, taking selected excerpts from millions of documents, and leaking them to the media selectively to give a distorted impression to the public. Williams was sued in September 1993 by the law firm employing him as a paralegal, claiming theft, fraud, conversion, breach of fiduciary and common law duties, and breach of contract (*Courier-Journal* 1997).

Dr. Stanton Glantz and a team of scientists examined the B&W documents and wrote about them in a series of articles in the *Journal of the American Medical Association*. Remarking on the importance of the documents, Dr. Glantz said on the CBS television program *60 Minutes* that "the documents told me that 30 years ago, B&W and British American Tobacco, its parent, knew nicotine was an addictive drug and they knew smoking caused cancer and other diseases" (*60 Minutes* 1996).

Dr. Jeffrey Wigand's Whistleblowing Experiences

Dr. Jeffrey Wigand was vice president of research and development (R&D) for the B&W Tobacco Corporation from January 1989 to late March 1993. B&W is the nation's third largest tobacco company. As the senior officer in R&D, Dr. Wigand was responsible for reporting to, consulting with, and giving advice to Thomas Sandefur, the president of B&W. Wigand said in court testimony that during his employment at B&W his previous job performance reviews were "above average" and that he received the Quality Leadership Award from his research colleagues at B&W. By the end of his employment, Wigand was in charge of approximately 243 scientists and workers in the R&D unit, with operating expenses of up to $30 million and capital expenses between $4 and $7 million (Wigand 1995). His annual salary was about $400,000. Dr. Wigand has a Ph.D. in biochemistry and endocrinology and was previously employed in the pharmaceutical and biomedical industry.

In a much publicized and anticipated segment of the CBS program *60 Minutes* that was initially delayed by fear of legal action, Dr. Wigand said that one of the reasons he was hired by B&W was to make a safer cigarette that would reduce the carcinogens within tobacco products (*60 Minutes* 1996). After a discussion of "safer" cigarettes with other scientists who worked for British American Tobacco Companies, however, Wigand noticed that a staff attorney at B&W rewrote the minutes of the meeting, editing out and toning down discussions of the safer cigarette. Wigand testified in court records that staff lawyers would pre-read and edit documents that considered sensitive issues such as biological research, safer cigarettes, or poisonous substances. Wigand also claimed that the fear of product liability suits from acknowledging a "safer" cigarette (implying that other tobacco products are "unsafe") was the primary reason he was told by company president Sandefur that there would be no further discussions or efforts at B&W to develop this product.

After abandoning his idea of trying to develop a new and safer cigarette, Wigand told *60 Minutes,* he turned his attention to investigating the additives and flavoring in B&W tobacco products. Wigand alleged that one of these flavorings, coumarin, was used in B&W's pipe tobacco products even after it was shown to cause various cancers. When he sent a memo to Sandefur voicing his concerns about coumarin, Wigand remarked on the CBS program, he was told that B&W would continue working on a substitute for coumarin but wouldn't remove it because it would impact sales. After confronting Sandefur, the newly appointed CEO and ex-salesman, Wigand said that he wasn't surprised that he was fired (*60 Minutes* 1996). B&W denied Wigand's accusations and testified in court records that he was fired because he (1) misled management at B&W with half-truths to the point that management lost trust in him and (2) exhibited an abusive style with co-workers.

Dr. Wigand's identity as an external whistleblower became public after his termination at B&W. After his firing from the tobacco company, Wigand talked with investigators for the FDA about the tobacco industry in the spring of 1994. He testified in a civil investigation by the U.S. Department of Justice involving the industry's efforts to develop a "fire-safe cigarette." Dr. Wigand was designated as an expert in (1) a civil action in the state of Massachusetts, (2) a libel suit in Richmond, Virginia, and (3) a *Philip Morris vs. American Broadcasting Corporation* lawsuit. Aside from his controversial appearance on *60 Minutes*, Wigand was also a major witness in multistate lawsuits brought against the tobacco industry seeking reimbursement for the cost of smoking-related illnesses, and he was the star witness in the U.S. Justice Department's criminal investigation of B&W.

Dr. Wigand has made the following allegations against his former employer in court documents, newspaper coverage, and television interviews:

- B&W manipulated nicotine levels in cigarettes by the use of additives, by blending techniques, and by looking at genetically engineered tobacco. The primary form of managing or manipulating nicotine delivery was through the use of ammonia compounds. B&W knowingly put acetaldehyde, an additive that was used to boost the nicotine effect, in its tobacco products (Wigand 1995).

- B&W falsified evidence regarding the damaging effects of tobacco. Results of cigarette research were manipulated to prevent discovery in the event of litigation. Company lawyers edited potentially incriminating information out of company reports.
- Tobacco companies, knowing that nicotine was addictive before federal researchers did, deliberately manipulated nicotine levels in cigarettes to hook smokers.
- The public was intentionally misled to believe that the industry did not know tobacco was addictive or that there was a link between tobacco usage and disease. Former CEO Thomas Sandefur lied to the U.S. Congress when he said that he believed that nicotine was not addictive.
- B&W continued to use a flavoring in pipe tobacco that was known to cause cancer in lab animals.
- B&W quashed plans for developing a safer cigarette because of fear of litigation for "unsafe" tobacco products.

Retaliation for Whistleblowing

The nature of alleged retaliation against Dr. Wigand for disclosing industry practices has been wide, varied, and severe. It has involved physical threats against his family, lawsuits, negative publicity, and numerous threats of future litigation for speaking out.

Shortly after talking with the FDA about the tobacco industry, Dr. Wigand received two separate anonymous telephone calls that told him to "leave tobacco alone" and threatened his children. B&W denied any involvement with the alleged calls. Wigand told *60 Minutes* that he feared injury and started carrying a handgun after the phone calls.

On numerous occasions, Dr. Wigand has been threatened by B&W attorneys with lawsuits for such activities as breach of contract and a nondisclosure settlement agreement, divulging trade secrets, theft, fraud, and violating a temporary restraining order. B&W has served Wigand twice with lawsuits. In one case, the legal papers were handed to Wigand in a highly visible manner in a parking lot while he was leaving the high school property where he worked. His severance package with B&W, including salary and health care benefits, was temporarily cut off when B&W first initiated a lawsuit against Wigand for his disclosures. This lawsuit was settled and the benefits reinstated after Wigand agreed to sign a more restrictive, lifelong confidentiality agreement (*60 Minutes* 1996).

B&W also sued Wigand in November 1995, alleging that he violated confidentiality agreements and divulged company secrets. Wigand in a counterlawsuit accused B&W of portraying him in a false light and invading his privacy by compiling and disseminating reports of his past. In exchange for Wigand's dropping his lawsuit, B&W agreed to end a lengthy session of depositions it had been taking of Wigand to build a case against him (*News-Journal* [Daytona

Beach, Florida] 1997). The excessive use of legal proceedings such as depositions is often an effective way to threaten and harass less powerful opponents.

As part of an apparent campaign to discredit the whistleblower, B&W in January 1996 issued a five-hundred-page dossier entitled "The Misconduct of Jeffrey S. Wigand Available in the Public Record." This document alleged that Wigand had engaged in various types of misconduct, including an arrest for shoplifting, accusations of spousal abuse, and résumé-padding (CNN 1996). Federal prosecutors initiated a grand jury probe to determine whether B&W was trying to intimidate Wigand with the intent to deter him from testifying against the company (CNN 1996). Subsequent investigations by the *Wall Street Journal* indicated that many of the serious allegations against Dr. Wigand in the dossier were backed by scanty or contradictory evidence.

Finally, during his deposition in a lawsuit brought by the state of Mississippi against the tobacco industry, Wigand was repeatedly told by a B&W lawyer of the possibility of legal action for his breach of confidentiality agreements and divulging trade secrets. Similar actions were taken by B&W toward Dr. Wigand upon gaining knowledge of his meeting with *60 Minutes*. Compared to the other whistleblowers I have studied, the scope and nature of apparent retaliation against Dr. Wigand have been far more dramatic and chronic.

Consequences of Whistleblowing

By all accounts, Dr. Jeffrey Wigand's testimony about B&W practices has had a dramatic impact on public policy and public attitudes toward the tobacco industry. Through the disclosures by Dr. Wigand and Merrell Williams, the FDA acquired the information it needed to regulate tobacco by establishing rules that would govern the accessibility of cigarettes and designate nicotine as a drug. The attorneys general in more than half of the U.S. states now had crucial information to use to sue the tobacco industry for reimbursements for the costs of smoking-related illnesses. From the perspective of antitobacco activists, the timing of these disclosures was nearly perfect because it occurred a short period after the seven U.S. tobacco companies testified under oath in a U.S. congressional hearing that they did not believe that nicotine is addictive or dangerous and that their companies did not manipulate its levels (*Courier-Journal* 1997). As of January 1998, there were more than forty major lawsuits against the tobacco industry. Contrary to previous statements by these officials, the CEOs of all the major tobacco companies now acknowledge that nicotine is an addictive drug. The B&W files contributed to a critical mass of documentation against the tobacco industry and provided the catalyst for litigation and future investigation of industry practices.

Aftermath of Whistleblowing

Although the tobacco industry has been sent into a tailspin by the allegations by Dr. Wigand and the ongoing legal battles, much has happened to the messenger in the aftermath of his disclosures. Aside from the various types of retaliation he believes the tobacco industry has inflicted on him, Dr. Wigand's life has changed in several fundamental ways. First, his marriage was dissolved, and his former wife received sole custody of his children. Second, some of his attorneys have filed a lawsuit against him for failing to pay their legal fees. Third, his salary has dropped from $400,000 per year as a major executive to slightly more than $30,000 as a high school teacher. Fourth, he remains in constant jeopardy of future legal action by tobacco officials for unlawful disclosures.

Given these extreme and adverse consequences, however, it is somewhat amazing that Dr. Wigand remains steadfast in his convictions. On the day of the historic $368.5 billion settlement agreed to by the tobacco industry for reimbursing states' medical expenses, Wigand was quoted in the *New York Times* as saying that he would do it again. Although at times he expressed reservations about this action, he also told *60 Minutes* that "I think it's worth it. I think in the end people will see the truth" (*60 Minutes* 1996).

Summary

The whistleblowers portrayed in this chapter are probably atypical in the gravity of misconduct they have reported, the impact of their disclosures on the quality of their lives, and the nature and length of their litigation histories. Nonetheless, their stories are important because they convey how successful whistleblowing can be accomplished and highlight the hazards of taking this action. For Mike Quint, Trudi Lytle, Helen Frost and the John Does at Area 51, Norm Buske, Mark O'Neal, and Jeffrey Wigand, whistleblowing has involved enormous personal risks with mixed discernible rewards. Other whistleblowers have received greater external rewards and vindication for their efforts.

The next chapter is designed to provide a general guide to whistleblowing. It outlines pivotal points and key issues that potential whistleblowers should consider when making the decision to report organizational and occupational misconduct.

8

Strategic Choices
and Practical Advice

The decision to blow the whistle on organizational misconduct is never easy or clear-cut. There are risks and rewards for both speaking out and remaining silent. Whatever choice is made, there are consequences for the individual, the organization, and the wider society. Most whistleblowers discover that exposing organizational misconduct is a low-reward and high-risk activity. In hindsight, many whistleblowers also second-guess their actions, saying they "should have" done this or that. So, before you act, it's important to realize that exposing abuse and corruption is serious business that has lifelong consequences.

As a general guide for potential whistleblowers, this final chapter summarizes major issues and strategic choices involved in the whistleblowing process. The unpredictability of the reactions from the organization, co-workers, and the legal system makes it unrealistic and foolish to think that there is a perfect way to report misconduct. Nonetheless, by considering various situational and organizational factors, potential whistleblowers may be better informed and advised of their strategic choices about (1) what misconduct to report, (2) how to report it and to whom, (3) how to exercise legal remedies for retaliatory actions, and (4) what to expect in the aftermath of whistleblowing. Being prepared and able to anticipate the reactions to your disclosures is fundamental for escaping relatively unscathed from the whistleblowing experience.

What Misconduct to Report

The triggering event for all whistleblowing is the initial misconduct. This misconduct varies widely in type, seriousness, frequency of occurrence, characteristics of the violator, importance to organizational survival, and whether the whistleblower is protected from retaliation for reporting it. Potential whistleblowers must decide whether the conduct is worth reporting. Here are some general observations that may influence this decision.

Occupational Versus Organizational Misconduct

There is a fundamental difference in the reactions for reporting occupational and organizational misconduct. By definition, organizational misconduct furthers the goals of the organization. Among these activities, the reporting of organizational crimes that are both frequent in occurrence and imperative for organizational success will elicit the most severe and swift retaliatory actions. However, the reporting of any type of organizational misconduct will be viewed critically because it violates the norms of silence within organizations and indicates that these "squealers" cannot be trusted to remain quiet about future organizational abuses.

Occupational misconduct, in contrast, involves activities that are committed for personal gain and not generally supported by the organization. Employee theft, counterproductive work activities (such as leaving work early or drug and alcohol use on the job), and many prohibited personnel practices (such as sexual harassment and racial discrimination in promotion or firing decisions) are examples of occupational misconduct. Unless the reporting of occupational misconduct reflects poorly upon the entire organization, whistleblowing is generally safer on this activity. However, the person accused of occupational misconduct will become an instant enemy of the whistleblower, doing whatever is necessary to discredit the source and mess with the whistleblower's life. Regardless of what conduct is reported, whistleblowers should expect some form of retaliation for their disclosures.

Characteristics of the Offending Party

Before deciding to report misconduct, it is prudent to evaluate the violator. Is the offender a key figure in the organization? Does the violator have more standing and/or better connections to the power base within the organization than the potential whistleblower? Is upper management already aware of the misconduct and supportive of it? When all things are considered, who will be supported by the organization: the offender or the whistleblower?

As is the case with attempts to expose hidden ownership in the corporate business world, it may be difficult in some cases to figure out how connected a particular offender is to the organization. Nonetheless, potential whistleblowers would be strongly advised to investigate more closely the offender's relative position and contacts within the organization prior to a decision to report either occupational or organizational misconduct. In general, allegations about members of the proverbial "old boy" network are more likely to elicit reprisals than disclosures about offenders who are less entrenched in the organizational structure.

Is Reporting This Misconduct Protected?

Before making any commitment to reporting misconduct, it is important to know whether your actions are legally protected against reprisals. In other words, what legal safeguards do you have if you report this particular misconduct?

As described in Chapter 6, whistleblowers are protected against retaliation by the U.S. Constitution, federal and state statutes, and the common law in each state. This protection, however, is uneven and unpredictable, focusing on disclosures of particular information to particular sources. Whether any particular disclosure of wrongdoing is protected under the First Amendment, for example, depends on a case-by-case analysis (Kohn and Kohn 1988:18). In the absence of proof that false statements are made knowingly or recklessly, individuals have the right under the First Amendment to speak on issues of "public importance." Under both federal and state statutes, protection is often restricted to *particular* types of workers who disclose *particular* types of violations of laws and rules (e.g., substantial misconduct) in a *particular* sequence to *particular* agents. Exceptions to the at-will termination doctrine have been established in most states' common law when retaliatory actions are designed to contravene a public policy, but what qualifies as protective actions varies by state. In each of these legal arenas, whether a particular disclosure of misconduct will be protected is uncertain and subject to multiple interpretations.

At this initial stage of the whistleblowing process, it is important to think carefully before you act and to know your options. Rather than relying upon internal sources (such as the personnel office, union officials, or ombudsman) for legal advice on whether a particular disclosure is protected, there are several outside resources that are available to assist whistleblowers in determining their legal rights. These include (1) various watchdog groups that provide some information and technical assistance to whistleblowers (see Appendix), (2) public libraries that contain the current state and federal statutes, and (3) lawyers with expertise in the areas of employee rights. With proper knowledge of one's legal protection, a more rational decision can be made about whether and how to report organizational and occupational misconduct.

The Motivation for Reporting

Before reporting any misconduct, it's also important to ask why you are doing it. Is the motivation revenge for previous abuses, the defense of a strong moral principle such as justice, or the protection of the public health and safety? Given the poor success record for most whistleblowers, persons motivated purely by revenge and retribution may be extremely disappointed in the majority of cases. In contrast, whistleblowers motivated by a desire to protect the public good or safety may elicit greater public support for their actions and reap greater personal satisfaction from their disclosures even when it does not change organizational practices. No one in the abstract can determine whether their actions are worth it, but revenge is rarely sweet in the long struggle that faces the typical whistleblower.

How to Report Misconduct

A number of strategic choices need to be made about how to report misconduct. These involve (1) anonymous reporting of misconduct, (2) the reporting channels that should be followed, (3) the relative advantages of internal and external reporting, and (4) the involvement of the mass media and external regulatory bodies.

Anonymous Reporting and the Use of Hot Lines

An increasingly common administrative tool for reporting problems within organizations is the development of hot lines and suggestion boxes. From management's perspective, such reporting channels help expose misconduct at work and keep the activity from becoming public. From the employee's perspective, hot lines and suggestion boxes provide an anonymous arena in which to voice concerns about organizational practices. Unfortunately, hot lines have an abysmal track record in terms of investigation of allegations, substantiation of charges, and corrective action (GAP 1997b). Recent court action also suggests that highly sensitive disclosures on "anonymous" hot lines run by the corporate ombudsman can be made public information

(*Business Week* 1997). Although hot lines may be somewhat cathartic for whistleblowers as a mechanism to vent their frustrations, they are not usually a safe or reliable channel for whistleblowers who are concerned with making constructive changes in organizational practices.

There are clear advantages of anonymous reporting for whistleblowers. It minimizes the chances of retaliation, there is less intense public scrutiny of the whistleblower, and less time and energy are expended on filing witness statements, gathering corroborating evidence, and testifying in administrative proceedings. Unfortunately, the major disadvantage of anonymous reporting is that such reports are often viewed as less credible and are not investigated as seriously as complaints filed by a known party. In addition, anonymous reporting is impossible in many work settings because the nature of the problem is only known to a select number of employees. Even when disclosures are made under the strictest standards of anonymity and confidentiality, it is amazing how frequently the whistleblower's identity becomes public knowledge (see GAP 1997b). "Deep Throat" in the Watergate scandal is one of the few exceptions to this general rule.

The decision to remain anonymous or not depends on the nature of the misconduct and the purpose for whistleblowing. When independent corroborating evidence of the wrongdoing is available from multiple sources, anonymous reporting offers greater protection for the whistleblower and still fulfills the desire to expose misconduct at work. Anonymous reporting is also the preferred strategy when the goal is to simply stir up trouble through individual or organizational sabotage. In contrast, if the employee desires constructive changes in organizational practices, direct disclosure of the whistleblower's identity is often required to validate the allegations and to help carry on the long battle for corrective action. Anonymous whistleblowing may also provide significant changes in organizational practices, but the "known" whistleblower who fights abuse and corruption at great personal costs is often a more sympathetic and effective champion for social change within organizations.

Reporting Channels

Most modern work organizations are hierarchical in structure with a well-defined chain of command. Workers are expected to file all complaint or general correspondence through the proper reporting channels. Complaints filed out of sequence will, on many occasions, be redirected to the appropriate administrative unit with little loss of continuity. In other cases, however, violation of the sacred reporting structure may nullify the complaint entirely.

Whistleblowers are in a rather unique position because following appropriate channels may not be in their best interest. Reporting misconduct by the "book" may lead to more general and widespread reprisals from multiple sources than may occur if the misconduct is reported directly at the onset to the CEO. Unfortunately, going to the top first may elicit swift and severe reprisals for both reporting misconduct *and* violating the sacred chain of command. Whistleblowers in some cases may be able to insulate themselves from certain retaliation by following appropriate channels and enlisting the wider support of co-workers and junior executives. Personnel directors and union representatives may be allies or

opponents, depending upon their history within this particular work environment and the whistleblower's special relationship with them.

Regardless of the nature of the misconduct, the first reporting channel should be family members and close
friends. Don't assume that ignorance is bliss for them or
that they are totally burned out listening to your work
problems. You will need their support and guidance because whatever you decide to do will also affect them. Marital conflict and strained interpersonal relationships are a
common consequence of whistleblowing, possibly because
these "significant others" are not included in the initial de-
liberation process. By being up front with immediate
friends and family, you can minimize much of the stress
and strain involved in whistleblowing and its aftermath.

Whether or not you should discuss organizational abuses
with friends who are co-workers, however, is less clear. Obviously, this decision depends on the level of your friendship and how well you believe that co-workers can be
trusted. Unfortunately, interviews with whistleblowers often reveal that co-workers are not a strong source of support or encouragement during their whistleblowing ordeal.
This is the case because many of the friendship ties among
co-workers are rather superficial, with only a thin line sepa-
rating interpersonal trust and its betrayal. In the worst-case
scenario of the "dog eat dog" world of modern business,
your closest friend at work may easily become your worst
enemy. Placing too much trust and faith in co-workers under these conditions may not be a wise move.

After discussions with family, close friends, and trusted
co-workers, the typical whistleblower will report miscon-

duct to an immediate supervisor or another appropriate representative within the company (such as personnel office, union representative, ombudsman). It is important to emphasize, however, that most of these people are not neutral parties. Rather, they have a clear vested interest in maintaining the status quo and their relative position within it. When the battle invariably ensues between the whistleblower and the organization, will the personnel office or union representative be your friend or foe? Based on the experiences of previous whistleblowers, you should not expect a great deal of support from internal administrative channels.

An alternative strategy for reporting misconduct is the "shotgun" approach, illustrated by Mike Quint's disclosures about faulty construction in the Los Angeles subway tunnels. Rather than follow a linear progression from one investigative agency to another, the shotgun approach involves the reporting of misconduct to a wide array of internal and external agencies at the same time. The advantage of this approach is that it (1) increases the public visibility of organizational misconduct, (2) increases the chances that at least some agency will take corrective action, and (3) provides whistleblowers with potentially greater insulation against retaliation because they are now visible "public" figures. The disadvantage of this approach, however, is that the whistleblower may be (1) precluded from taking formal action because of having violated mandated reporting channels, (2) held liable under the legal categories of slander or defamation, and (3) considered merely a zealot and a less credible "victim."

Regardless of the reporting approach or strategy, however, whistleblowers are strongly advised to seek legal counsel early in the process to become fully aware of their legal rights and protection. Lawyers will know the current status of employment law in their state, statutory protection of whistleblowers, and constitutional safeguards. If contacted prior to reporting the misconduct, legal representatives may be able to provide advice on documentation of the allegations, gathering evidence, disclosure options, and estimates of the likely success of remedial actions. However, seeking good legal advice and getting it are often two different things. Accordingly, the whistleblower should perform a preliminary assessment of whether the attorney has handled similar cases in the past, is well respected within the legal profession, and has sufficient resources to fully investigate the allegations. If the misconduct involves the potential for large financial recoveries and payment of attorney fees, competent lawyers may be retained on a contingency basis. Various watchdog groups like GAP and Taxpayers Against Fraud (TAF) should be contacted early in the process for preliminary advice on legal protection and possible alternative courses of action.

Internal Versus External Reporting

The majority of whistleblowers restrict their disclosures to persons within the organization rather than to external sources. The prevalence of internal whistleblowing is a product of both preferences and standing. People prefer internal disclosure because it is less threatening to the organization and less likely to elicit reprisals. Others engage in internal whistleblowing simply because the misconduct does not involve public health and safety or is not serious enough to warrant external review. In many cases, internal whistleblowing is sufficient to curb wrongdoing within the organization, and external whistleblowing only occurs when these internal channels have failed to correct the situation.

The decision to go outside the organization for corrective action increases dramatically the risks and possible rewards for whistleblowing. Once you go public, you will feel the entire wrath of the organization. It is not uncommon for external whistleblowers to have their personal lives closely scrutinized for any kind of "dirt," to receive threatening phone calls, to have their possessions vandalized and destroyed, and to be subjected to separate investigations by law enforcement officials. In the case of major financial fraud and corruption, whistleblowing is serious business, and the affected organization will spare little expense to discredit and nullify the whistleblower. If you are disclosing this type of organizational misconduct to external agents, be prepared for a long and stressful process.

When internal disclosures result in retaliatory action, external whistleblowing is often the only available means for achieving restitution and compensation. Internal grievance boards within organizations rarely support whistleblowers over management and, in the rare case that they do, offer little relief beyond reinstatement. By definition, external reporting is required for compensatory damages through civil lawsuits and for monetary awards to whistleblowers under special legislation like the False Claims Act. If the whistleblower is seeking financial benefits for reporting misconduct or for retaliatory actions against them, some level of external whistleblowing is necessary.

CALL NO. COMPUTER #06Checkout Receipt
A-B Tech Community College
04/21/08 01:05PM
****
PATRON: 23312000412645

Whistleblowing at work : tough choices i

Collection: abg
Call No: HD 60.5 .U5 M54 1999
Barcode: 33312000697474
Due Time:
Due Date: 05/05/08

TOTAL: 1Checkout Receipt
A-B Tech Community College
04/21/08 01:05PM
****
PATRON: 23312000412645

Whistleblowing at work : tough choices i

Collection: abg
Call No: HD 60.5 .U5 M54 1999
Barcode: 33312000697474
Due Time:
Due Date: 05/05/08

It is important to realize, however, that not all external sources are equally useful for reporting organizational misconduct. Different external agents, regulatory bodies, legislators, and law enforcement officials should be evaluated on their relative track records prior to whistleblowing. Although nonprofit groups and media sources are often considered the most effective reporting channels (GAP 1997b), whether you should utilize these sources depends on the particular misconduct and the particular reputations of these reporting bodies.

The Involvement of Mass Media and External Regulatory Bodies

The mass media are incredible resources for exposing corruption and increasing the credibility of a whistleblower's allegations. Through investigative reporting and mass publicity, the media have great power to apply pressure on governmental regulatory agencies, law enforcement officials, and local politicians to step up their own investigations. However, each of these external bodies has its own agenda, which is not necessarily in the best interest of the whistleblower. Although the media and external regulatory bodies have enormous potential to expose and control organizational misconduct, there is no guarantee that these organizations will be helpful in your particular whistleblowing situation. If these external sources are utilized, persistence on your part will keep the issue alive and help prevent the complaint from becoming lost in the abyss of governmental and organizational bureaucracies.

Another major external source for whistleblowing is the U.S. Congress. Particular members may have enormous clout to raise public awareness of the organizational misconduct and apply pressure to take corrective action. As with any other source, however, potential whistleblowers must do their homework to determine an elected official's track record, constituency base, and particular political and social ties. When contacting members of Congress, GAP (1997b: 73–75) provides the following tips on how to establish contact and work successfully with these political officials:

- Before you write to members of Congress, make sure that you have thoroughly checked their track record. Have they helped whistleblowers in the past and followed up once the headlines faded?
- Keep your letter short. If it is impossible to condense your letter to two pages or less, it is a good idea to prepare a one-page fact sheet or an executive summary.
- Make it clear early in your letter whether you consent to having your name or documents shared with anyone in the bureaucracy. Make it clear to your reader whether or not you need to remain anonymous.
- In a clear and concise way, state your factual case in the beginning. Keep your story clear of jargon and do not assume that the staff member who reads the letter will understand how your agency or company works.
- Focus on the public-interest issues raised by your allegations.
- Offer guidance for follow-through. At the end of your letter, make suggestions on where congres-

sional staff might go to pursue follow-up investigations or further corroborating documents.

- Make sure that staff members have a way to reach you during their working hours. If you can't talk to them from your workplace, find a discreet way for someone to take a message for you and return the call from an outside telephone during your lunchtime.
- If you have not received a reply within two weeks, call the office in Washington and ask to speak to the legislative assistant who covers your issue areas. Do not be a pest, but make sure that you do not fall through the cracks.
- Offer to act as a "ghost writer" in drafting communications for congressional staffers who are open to pursuing your allegations and are interested in a working relationship with you.
- Watchdog groups have good working relationships with various members of Congress, and you may be more successful going through them. These watchdog groups can play the role of advocate for you and sometimes can keep your identity anonymous.

The Inspector General Act of 1978 created special offices within most federal agencies that are responsible for investigating and reporting misconduct by its employees or the agency itself. As a channel for reporting abuses, however, offices of inspectors general in a number of governmental agencies have been criticized for breaching the whistleblower's confidentiality and spending more time searching for information to discredit and retaliate against the whistleblower than in compiling and investigating the evidence of misconduct (GAP 1997b). In general, these external regulatory agencies are inherently tied to the offending organization and often provide little vindication or relief for whistleblowers.

Legal Remedies for Retaliatory Action

Few whistleblowers expose organizational misconduct without adverse personal consequences. Instead, the typical external whistleblower usually faces swift, severe, and multiple forms of individual and organizational retaliation. These actions include job termination and demotion, reassignment to other tasks and locations, denial of promotions and raises, verbal and physical harassment, threat of termination of employment benefits, greater monitoring of work performance, changes in workload expectations, exclusion from central employment activities, blacklisting and the denial of employment opportunities in other locations, and criticism and avoidance by co-workers. Rates of retaliatory action are lower for internal whistleblowers, but they experience the same type of reprisals.

Even though federal and state laws protect many whistleblowers from retaliatory actions, this protection is usually restricted to retaliatory discharge or termination of employment. The more subtle forms of reprisal against whistleblowers are not covered under these legal remedies. For example, the following unprotected retaliatory actions have been experienced by whistleblowers I have interviewed: (1) reassignment to a physical location without windows and about the size of a standard closet, (2) relocation of the work desk so that the employee is always working in direct sunlight, and (3) removal of privacy barriers in work stations so that the whistleblower's behavior can be more closely monitored.

Even in the case of retaliatory discharge, however, having legal protection in theory may not translate into legal protection in actual practice. In fact, whistleblowers are rarely successful in their legal action against organizations. To increase the chances of successful litigation, whistleblowers must have clear documentation of wrongful treatment, sufficient evidence that their whistleblowing was a primary motive for discriminatory treatment, and adequate legal counsel to make sure their particular legal rights are protected.

The Lawyer's Responsibilities

If you are serious about reporting misconduct, legal representation is needed as soon as possible. Legal counsel is necessary to determine whether your particular whistleblowing situation is actually covered under abstract legal rules and codes. Your attorney also has several strategic choices to make in terms of how to best represent your case. According to Kohn and Kohn (1988:74–76), your attorney should consider the following specific actions and issues:

- Identify what statute or common law action provides a remedy and the best remedy, because the case may be covered by more than one whistleblower protection provision.
- Review the statute of limitations for filing this particular complaint under the particular statute.

- Determine whether common law action (such as a civil suit for damages) is preempted or precluded by a preexisting statutory remedy.
- Assess what impact, if any, the filing of an administrative complaint has on a potential state common law action.
- Determine whether the case contains facts or issues that are not suitable for an administrative body or a jury evaluating the facts and awarding damages.
- Discuss with the client his or her willingness to underwrite the costs of a long, grueling suit and assess whether other administrative procedures are more economical and practical.
- Identify the legal forum that is most appropriate for airing a public policy concern raised by the whistle-blowing activity.
- Provide a reasonable estimate of the amount of time that a final determination will take in this particular forum.
- Ascertain the risks of simultaneously filing in multiple forums.
- Evaluate whether there are other forums or laws through which to pursue the whistleblower's claim.

If your complaint of wrongful discharge goes to court, your attorney will have to prove the basic prima facie case and rebut management's defense that the discharge and other discriminatory practices were for legitimate business reasons. The basic components of the prima facie case to be proven include the following elements: (1) The plaintiff is an employee protected under this specific statute or common law principle; (2) the plaintiff engaged in a protected whistleblower activity; (3) the defendant had knowledge that the plaintiff engaged in such activity; (4) the retaliatory actions against the plaintiff were motivated, at least in part, by the employee's engaging in the protected activity; (5) the plaintiff was discharged or otherwise discriminated against with respect to compensation, terms, conditions, or privileges of employment; and (6) the plaintiff acted in good faith when he or she engaged in the protected activity (Kohn and Kohn 1988:76–77).

As evidence of the defendant's discriminatory motive, your attorney will draw upon changes in your work experiences and performance evaluations after the whistleblowing event. Evidence to support a "reasonable inference" of discriminatory treatment includes hostile attitudes, disparaging treatment, the emergence of negative performance evaluations, the manner in which the employee is informed of termination or transfer decisions, the specific timing of these activities, and documentation of the relative treatment of the whistleblower compared with other employees similarly situated within the organization (Kohn and Kohn 1988:77).

The Aftermath of Whistleblowing

Whistleblowing has long-term consequences for the individual whistleblower, the offending organization, and the wider society. These consequences are positive and negative.

For many whistleblowers, the experience of reporting organizational misconduct results in a substantial transformation of their lives. The struggle with reporting misconduct, the loss of faith and trust in major institutions, family disruption, declining physical and psychological well-being, diminished loyalty and confidence in co-workers, and widespread feelings of alienation and powerlessness create a situation in which the whistleblowing event becomes a "master status" and overpowers nearly all other aspects of a person's life. Most whistleblowers are permanently scarred by the process and hold bitter memories about the experience. Vindication for whistleblowing only occurs when the corrupt practices are fully exposed and the offending individual or organization is forced to take corrective action.

For the organization involved in serious misconduct, whistleblowers may derail a near-perfect immunity from public scrutiny. External whistleblowing may have some benefits to the organization (for instance, helping them identify "bad apples"), but usually business organizations are fearful of the reports by whistleblowers and do whatever is necessary to undermine their credibility. As for the effectiveness of whistleblowing, public disclosures rarely result in major changes in organizational practices. Only the threat of civil action under the False Claims Act appears to be a major deterrent for organizational misconduct.

From the perspective of wider society, whistleblowing may contribute to declining productivity in work organizations and the overmonitoring of employees' activities, but it remains a necessary social control measure in modern society. Without the disclosures from whistleblowers, we would have limited means of exposing and subsequently controlling organizational abuses. As public servants, whistleblowers are uniquely situated to maintain accountability and protect the public good within modern work settings.

Under these conditions, the potential whistleblower must weigh the relative personal, organizational, and societal costs and benefits from exposing misconduct at work. Family members, close friends, and legal representatives may help potential whistleblowers make rational decisions about speaking out or remaining silent. Although most whistleblowing is a low-reward and high-cost activity for the whistleblower, those who decide to expose organizational misconduct are often providing an enormous public service.

A Checklist of Questions
for Potential Whistleblowers

Although people often want clear and decisive answers to their questions, there are only two definitive conclusions about whistleblowing. First, whistleblowing in modern society has both costs and rewards. Second, the decision to report organizational misconduct needs to be considered within the context of the particular misconduct and the organization in which it occurs. By answering the following questions about your personal life and work experiences, it is hoped that you as a potential whistleblower can make sound decisions about whether or not to report organizational misconduct.

Preparation for Whistleblowing

- Do you have documented physical evidence that serious misconduct took place? Do you have the right to have these documents and other physical evidence? Can the misconduct be corroborated through independent sources?

- Have you developed a "paper trail" to document (1) your efforts to resolve the problem through informal and nonadversarial ways and (2) the specific times and places where misconduct took place?
- Is management or the individual offender already suspicious of your activities? Can you copy supporting documents and other records without raising further suspicion?
- How deep within the organization is this misconduct? In other words, is the misconduct actively supported or encouraged across levels of management?
- Is disclosure of this wrongdoing to public sources protected under special security provisions? Is reporting this conduct a violation of national security or contractual conditions?
- Are other workers aware of the wrongdoing? If yes, what is their reaction to it?
- Would any of your co-workers be willing to risk their careers and come forward to support your actions?
- Have you thought clearly about the costs and benefits from reporting this wrongdoing?
- Have you talked with family members and close friends about this wrongdoing? What do they think you should do?
- Are you fully aware of your legal rights in this work setting? Is your whistleblowing protected by either the U.S. Constitution, federal or state law, or the state's common law? Do multiple, independent attorneys arrive at the same conclusion about your legal protection?

- Have you consulted with an attorney or watchdog organization to become fully knowledgeable of your legal rights?

Organizational Characteristics and Context

- Do you work in the public or private sector? Is the type of work you do in this organization protected under state or federal whistleblowing laws?
- Does your organization or company have a past record of retaliation against workers who speak out?
- Does this organization or company have a good reputation for protecting workers' rights?
- Are you a union employee? If so, how supportive is the union of whistleblowing and employee grievances?
- Do you have good working relationships with administrative and support staff who may "leak" you information or provide discreet warnings about upcoming organizational activities?
- What is the ethical or moral character of the administrative head or CEO? Does this person widely support the rights of employees?
- Does the organization or company have nearly exclusive control over business activities in the community? If yes, do they have the power to limit your employment opportunities elsewhere in the community?
- What is the relative position of the whistleblower and offender in the organization? Do you, as the

whistleblower, have less clout than the offending party? When all is said and done, who will management support, you or the accused?

- Does the misconduct in this organization involve fraudulent activities against federal programs or contracts? If so, is this covered under the False Claims Act?
- Is there an opportunity for anonymous whistleblowing in this work setting? Are there enough employees in the work setting who have observed the same misconduct that the whistleblower can remain anonymous? Is there a hot line that allows for anonymous reporting?

Personal Background and Resources

- Do you have the money to hire a good attorney? Do you know a good attorney?
- Do you have the financial resources to survive up to six months of unemployment?
- Do you have particular skills that are easily marketable in the event that you are fired?
- Are your spouse, significant others, and other family members in total support of your actions? Do they know what they are getting into?
- Do you have any "skeletons" in your closet that vindictive people and organizations could use against you?
- Are your company benefits and seniority vested— that is, can these benefits be taken away by a vindictive employer? Are you willing to give these up for disclosing organizational misconduct?

- Can you afford to lose this battle, both psychologically and economically?
- Can you detach your personal feelings from the facts of the case? How will you feel if you win? How about if you lose?
- Will your disclosures make a difference in organizational practices?

Conclusion

Whistleblowing is a tough decision that has both positive and negative consequences. Regardless of what you do, the decision to speak out or remain silent will often affect both your personal life and professional career. The hope is that consideration of some of the issues addressed in this book will enable potential whistleblowers to better make informed decisions and minimize the adverse personal consequences of exposing fraud, waste, and abuse at work.

Appendix

Support Organizations and
Resources for Whistleblowers

There are a growing number of support organizations and resources for whistleblowers across the country. These sources vary in their particular services and the type of employees that are covered. Federal employees and private workers in specific industries have access to hot lines and particular support organizations. For all potential whistleblowers, however, a growing listing of support organizations and resources is available on the World Wide Web. A keyword search of the word *whistleblowing* or *whistleblower* on the Internet will provide the most current listing of these resources. The most widely known support organizations for whistleblowers are summarized below.

The Government Accountability Project

The most visible support organization for whistleblowers is the Government Accountability Project (GAP). This organization has provided legal advice and assistance to thousands of citizens who expose wrongdoing involving threats to the public health and the environment (GAP 1997b). Although only a small proportion of whistleblowers who contact GAP receive legal representation by staff attorneys, all callers are given some general assistance. GAP staff have developed an expertise in the following policy areas: (1) strengthening the rights and protections of whistleblowers, (2) ensuring a safe and cost-effective cleanup at nuclear weapons facilities, (3) increasing food safety, (4) enforcing environmental protection laws, and (5) curtailing national security abuses (GAP 1997b:159–160). The current address for this organization is:

Government Accountability Project
1612 K Street NW, Suite 400
Washington, DC 20006
Phone: (202) 408-0034
Fax: (202) 408-9855
Internet: www.whistleblower.org/gap

Project on Government Oversight

The Project on Government Oversight (POGO) is a watchdog organization designed to investigate, expose, and remedy abuses of power, mismanagement, and government subservience to special interests (GAP 1997b:161). POGO has performed independent investigations of specific issues and worked with whistleblowers to monitor and report cases of fraud, waste, and abuse within federal agencies. For additional information about this Washington-based organization, contact them by phone (202-466-5539) or Internet (www.mnsinc.com/pogo).

Taxpayers Against Fraud

Taxpayers Against Fraud (TAF) is a nonprofit public interest organization that promotes and disseminates information concerning the False Claims Act and *qui tam* lawsuits. TAF works with a variety of *qui tam* attorneys throughout the country and publishes *False Claims Act and Qui Tam Quarterly Review*, a report that overviews case decisions, settlements, and other developments involving the False Claims Act (TAF 1997b). For additional information about this organization, call TAF at 202-296-4826.

Cited Studies and General References

Akerstrom, Malin. 1991. *Betrayal and Betrayers: The Sociology of Treachery.* New Brunswick, NJ: Transaction Publishers.

Bayer, Alan E., Deborah Strickland, and Terance D. Miethe. 1992. *Quality of Life in Virginia: 1992.* Blacksburg: Center for Survey Research, Virginia Polytechnic Institute and State University.

Blackburn, M. S. 1988. Employee dissent: The choice of voice or silence. Ph.D. diss., University of Tennessee, Knoxville.

BNA [Bureau of National Affairs]. 1995. *BNA Labor Relations Reporter Manual.* Vols. 4, 4A, 9A. Washington, DC: BNA.

_____. 1996. *BNA Labor Relations Reporter Manual.* Vols. 4, 4A, 9A. Washington, DC: BNA.

_____. 1997. *BNA Labor Relations Reporter Manual.* Vols. 4, 4A, 9A. Washington, DC: BNA.

Bowman, James S., Frederick Elliston, and Paula Lockhart. 1984. *Professional Dissent: An Annotated Bibliography and Resource Guide.* New York: Garland.

Brief, A. P., and S. J. Motowidlo. 1986. Prosocial organizational behaviors. *Academy of Management Review* 11:710–725.

Business Week. 1997. Now, the dirty laundry gets washed in public: An appeals court rules that ombudsmen can't keep their records secret. October 27.

Campbell, Glenn. 1993. *Area 51 Viewer's Guide.* Somerville, MA.

Chronicle of Higher Education. 1989. In Box. January 25.

Clift, Elayne. 1992. Women whistleblowers: What they say, the price they pay. *On the Issues* (Winter):18–21.

Clinard, Marshall. 1983. *Corporate Ethics and Crime.* Beverly Hills, CA: Sage.

CNN [Cable Network News]. 1996. Feds to investigate B & W intimidation claims. February 6.

Cockerham, John M. 1989. Whistleblowing on U.S. defense contractors is out of control. *Aviation Week and Space Technology* (April 10):99–101.

Coleman, James W. 1994. *The Criminal Elite.* 3d ed. New York: St. Martin's Press.

_____. 1995. Respectable crimes. In *Criminology,* edited by Joseph F. Sheley, 249–269. Belmont, CA: Wadsworth.

Cording, Edward J., Paul De Marco, and John M. Hanson. 1994. *Investigation of Structural Integrity of Los Angeles Red Line Tunnels, Segment 1.* Los Angeles County Metropolitan Transportation Authority. February.

Courier-Journal (Louisville, Kentucky). 1997. Blowing the whistle on big tobacco: Wigand, Williams lifted secrecy's veil. May 25.

Davis, L. J. 1994. Big bad Ron. *BUZZ* (October):86–93, 124.

Dozier, Janelle Brinker, and Marcia P. Miceli. 1985. Potential predictors of whistleblowing: A prosocial behavior perspective. *Academy of Management Review* 10 (October):823–836.

Dworkin, Terry Morehead, and Janet Near. 1987. Whistleblowing statutes: Are they working? *American Business Law Journal* 25:241–264.

Executive. 1992. Whistle-blowers: Saint or snitch? January/February.

Feliu, Alfred G. 1990. Whistleblowing while you work. *Business and Society Review* (Winter):65–67.

Friedrichs, David O. 1996. *Trusted Criminals: White-Collar Crime in Contemporary Society.* Belmont, CA: Wadsworth.

Galanter, Marc. 1974. Why the 'haves' come out ahead: Speculations on the limits of legal change. *Law and Society Review* 9(1):95–160.

GAO [General Accounting Office]. 1988a. *GAO Fraud Hotline.* Washington, DC: GAO.

_____. 1988b. *Whistleblowers: Management of the Program to Protect Trucking Company Employees Against Reprisal.* Washington, DC: GAO.

_____. 1992. *Whistleblower Protection: Survey of Federal Employees on Misconduct and Protection from Reprisals.* Washington, DC: GAO.

GAP [Government Accountability Project]. 1997a. "Whistleblower of the Month." Available: http://www.accessone.com/gap.

_____. 1997b. *The Whistleblower's Survival Guide: Courage Without Martyrdom.* Washington, DC: Fund for Constitutional Government.

George Washington University. 1994. Press Release. August 2.

Glazer, Myron, and Penina Glazer. 1989. *The Whistleblowers: Exposing Corruption in Government and Industry.* New York: Basic Books.

Graham, Jill W. 1986. Principled organizational dissent: A theoretical essay. In *Research in Organizational Behavior,* vol. 8, edited by L. L. Cummings and B. M. Staff, 1–52. Greenwich, CT: JAI Press.

Green, Gary S. 1990. *Occupational Crime.* Chicago: Nelson Hall.

Hodson, Randy, and Teresa A. Sullivan. 1995. *The Social Organization of Work.* 2d ed. Belmont, CA: Wadsworth Publishing.

Hughes, Everett C. 1945. Dilemmas and contradictions of status. *American Journal of Sociology* 50:353–359.

Jos, Philip, Mark E. Tompkins, and Steven W. Hays. 1989. In praise of difficult people: A portrait of the committed whistleblower. *Public Administration Review* (November/December):552–561.

Keenan, John P., and David L. McLain. 1992. Whistleblowing: A conceptualization and model. Paper presented at the annual meeting of the National Academy of Management. Las Vegas, Nevada. August.

Kohn, Stephen M., and Michael D. Kohn. 1988. *The Labor Lawyer's Guide to the Rights and Responsibilities of Employee Whistleblowers.* New York: Quorum Books.

Larmer, Robert A. Whistleblowing and employee loyalty. *Journal of Business Ethics* 11:125–128.

Las Vegas Review Journal. 1993a. Students' "sickout" protests transfer of teacher turned whistle-blower. January 30.

———. 1993b. Thin tunnel walls make L.A. subways vulnerable to earthquakes. August 30.

———. 1993c. State to examine Stealth base for toxic fumes: A worker's widow says dioxins were burned at a base near the Nevada Test Site, with deadly effects. October 19.

———. 1993d. Air Force promises openness: A Nevada agency is investigating claims that open-pit burning poisoned workers at a secret base. October 23.

———. 1993e. State seeks evidence of burn pits: Officials plan to search documents and the site of an Air Force base for proof of toxic chemical burning. November 16.

———. 1994a. Lawsuit planned against secret base. March 10.

———. 1994b. Teacher awaiting day in court with school district: Trudi Lytle says she lost her teaching position for pointing out a discrepancy in an educational program. June 7.

_____. 1994c. Former local teacher's rights suit goes before federal jury: A $500,000 tab could hang in the balance if the woman proves the school district forced her out. June 28.

_____. 1994d. School official says changes were needed. June 30.

_____. 1994e. Teacher awarded $135,000: A jury decides in favor of the ex-instructor who said the school district retaliated because of her criticism. July 2.

_____. 1994f. Officials fight teacher's return: Administrators cite "hostile" atmosphere. July 16.

_____. 1994g. Former Groom Lake employees sue government: An action filed Monday alleges that U.S. agencies hid some waste violations at the Lincoln County base. August 16.

_____. 1994h. School board approves rule protecting whistle-blowers. October 26.

_____. 1994i. National security defense cut from Groom lawsuits. November 11.

_____. 1995. Teacher again suing school district: Trudi Lytle accuses employers of continual harassment. October 27.

_____. 1996. Groom Lake suit bounced. March 7.

Las Vegas Sun. 1994. School district says jury erred on teacher. July 19.

_____. 1996a. Judge shuts door on Area 51 action: TV station's request for secret data denied. January 23.

_____. 1996b. Judge releases Groom Lake files: Fed documents used in lawsuit made public. July 17.

_____. 1996c. Feds investigating burning of hazardous waste at Area 51. August 8.

Ling, Eric. 1991. Whistleblowing: Toward a sociological understanding. Paper presented at the annual meeting of the American Society of Criminology, San Francisco. November.

Los Angeles Times. 1993. Head of subway probe linked to tunnel designer. November 30.

Mars, Gerald. 1982. _Cheats at Work: An Anthropology of Workplace Crime._ London: Unwin Paperbacks.

Marx, Gary T. 1988. _Undercover: Police Surveillance in America._ Berkeley: University of California Press.

Miceli, Marcia P., and Janet P. Near. 1984. The relationships among beliefs, organizational position, and whistle-blowing status: A discriminant analysis. _Academy of Management Journal_ 27:687–705.

_____. 1988. Individual and situational correlates of whistleblowing. *Personnel Psychology* 41:267–282.

_____. 1990. Is there a whistleblowing personality? Personal variables that may be associated with whistleblowing. Working paper series (WPS 90–19), College of Business. Ohio State University.

_____. 1992. *Blowing the Whistle*. New York: Lexington Books.

Miethe, Terance D. 1994. Factors related to whistleblowing among nurses. Typescript at University of Nevada–Las Vegas.

Miethe, Terance D., and Wayne Label. 1995. A survey of external auditors' attitudes toward whistleblowing. Typescript at University of Nevada– Las Vegas.

Miethe, Terance D., and Richard C. McCorkle. 1997. Gang membership and criminal processing: A test of the "Master Status" concept. *Justice Quarterly* 14(3):407–428.

Miethe, Terance D., and Joyce Rothschild. 1993. Whistleblowing in the U.S.: Results from a national survey. Typescript at University of Nevada–Las Vegas.

_____. 1994. Whistleblowing and the control of organizational misconduct. *Sociological Inquiry* 64:322–347.

_____. 1995. The prevalence of whistleblowing among employees in nonprofit organizations. Typescript at University of Nevada–Las Vegas.

Moore, Charles A. 1987. Taming the giant corporation: Some cautionary remarks on the deterrability of corporate crime. *Crime and Delinquency* 33(2):379–402.

MSPB [Merit Systems Protection Board]. 1981. *Whistleblowing and the Federal Employee: Blowing the Whistle on Fraud, Waste, and Mismanagement—Who Does It and What Happens*. Washington, DC: U.S. Merit Systems Protection Board, Office of Merit Systems Review and Studies.

_____. 1984. *Blowing the Whistle in the Federal Government: A Comparative Analysis of 1980 and 1983 Survey Findings. A Report of the U.S. Merit Systems Protection Board*. Washington, DC: Office of Merit Systems Review and Studies.

_____. 1993. *Whistleblowing in the Federal Government: An Update*. A Report to the President and Congress of the United States by the U.S. Merit Systems Protection Board. Washington, DC: U.S. Government Printing Office.

Near, Janet P., and Marcia P. Miceli. 1985. Organizational dissidence: The case of whistleblowing. *Journal of Business Ethics* 4:1–16.

_____. 1988. *The Internal Auditor's Ultimate Responsibility: The Reporting of Sensitive Issues.* Altamonte Springs, FL: The Institute of Internal Auditors Research Foundation.

News-Journal (Daytona Beach, Florida). 1997. Whistle-blower agrees to drop lawsuit against Brown & Williamson. June 19.

The Observer (London). 1996. Nightmare in dreamland. July 14.

Perrucci, Robert M., R. M. Anderson, D. E. Schendel, and L. E. Tractman. 1980. Whistleblowing: Professionals' resistance to organizational authority. *Social Problems* 28:149–164.

Petersen, James C., and Dan Farrell. 1986. *Whistleblowing: Ethical and Legal Issues in Expressing Dissent.* Module Series in Applied Ethics. Dubuque, IA: Kendall/Hunt.

Phillips and Cohen. 1996. "A Whistleblower's Web Site." Available: http://www.whistleblowers.com.

Pontell, Henry N., Paul D. Jesilow, and Gilbert Geis. 1982. Policing physicians: Practitioner fraud and abuse in a government medical program. *Social Problems* 30:117–125.

Popular Science. 1994. Searching for the secrets of Groom Lake. March.

Project on Government Oversight. 1994. Second lawsuit filed against the government concerning super secret facility at Groom Lake. Press Release. August 16.

Rothschild, Joyce, and Terance D. Miethe. 1992. Whistleblowing as occupational deviance and dilemma. Paper presented at the annual meeting of the American Sociological Association, Pittsburgh, August 20–24, 1992.

_____. 1994. Whistleblowing as resistance in modern work organizations: The politics of revealing organizational deception and abuse. In *Resistance and Power in Organizations: Agency, Subjectivity, and the Labor Process,* edited by John Jermier, Walter Nord, and David Knights. London: Routledge, Kegan.

60 Minutes. 1996. A CBS News program interview with Dr. Jeffrey Wigand. February 4.

Statistical Abstracts of the United States. 1996. Washington, DC: U.S. Bureau of the Census.

TAF [Taxpayers Against Fraud]. 1995. *False Claims Act and Qui Tam Quarterly Review*. January.
_____. 1996. *False Claims Act and Qui Tam Quarterly Review*. January.
_____. 1997a. *False Claims Act and Qui Tam Quarterly Review*. Vol. 8. January.
_____. 1997b. *The 1986 False Claims Act Amendments. Tenth Anniversary*. 1986–1996. Washington, DC: The False Claims Act Legal Center.
Vaughan, Diane. 1983. *Controlling Unlawful Corporate Behavior*. Chicago: University of Chicago Press.
Vogel, Robert L. 1991. Deterrent effects of "whistleblower" lawsuits justify False Claims Act. *Aviation Week and Space Technology* (November 4):73–74.
Wall Street Journal. 1992. Tipsters telephoning ethics hotline can end up sabotaging their own jobs. August 28.
_____. 1995. Suits pit national security against environmental law. January 18, B3.
_____. 1996. Desert battle: Secret air base broke Hazardous-Waste Act, workers' suit alleges. February 8.
Washington Lawyer. 1996. The return of Qui Tam. September/October.
Washington Monthly. 1990. GAP's in your defense: Making the government more accountable isn't just a job for the General Accounting Office, the inspectors general, and congressional committees. Private organizations like the Government Accountability Project are important too. February.
Washington Post. 1997. Secrets under the sun: Out in the Nevada desert is Area 51, a military base so hush-hush it does not officially exist. Tell that to the widows of the men who died there. July 20, F1, F4.
Westin, Alan F. 1981. *Whistleblowing: Loyalty and Dissent in the Corporation*. New York: McGraw-Hill.
Westman, Daniel P. 1991. *Whistleblowing: The Law of Retaliatory Discharge*. Washington, DC: The Bureau of National Affairs.
Wigand, Jeffrey. 1995. "Deposition in Lawsuit Brought by the State of Mississippi Seeking Reimbursement for the Cost of Smoking-Related Illness." Available: http://www.gate.net/~jcannon/documents/wigand.html. November 29.

Index